MW01486891

A First Dictionary and Grammar of **Láadan**:

Second Edition

Suzette Haden Elgin

Edited by Diane Martin

Society for the Furtherance and Study of Fantasy and Science Fiction, Inc.
Box 1624
Madison, WI 53701-1624

Other Works by Suzette Haden Elgin

Fiction
The Communipaths
Furthest
At the Seventh Level
Star-Anchored, Star-Angered
Twelve Fair Kingdoms
The Grand Jubilee
And then There'll be Fireworks
Yonder Comes the Other End of Time
Native Tongue
Native Tongue II: The Judas Rose

Non-Fiction
Guide to Transformational Grammar (with John Grinder)
What is Linguistics?, 1st Edition
Pouring Down Words
What is Linguistics?, 2nd Edition
The Gentle Art of Verbal Self-Defense
More on the Gentle Art of Verbal Self-Defense
The Last Word on the Gentle Art of Verbal Self-Defense

**The Society for the Furtherance and Study
of Fantasy and Science Fiction, Inc. (SF³)**
Box 1624
Madison, WI 53701-1624

Second Edition, March 1988
ISBN 0-9618641-0-9

Cover Design: Georgie Schnobrich
Interior Design & Production: Diane Martin
Illustrations are from *Women: A Pictorial Archive from Nineteenth-Century Sources*, compiled and
selected by Jim Harter, 2nd, revised edition (1982); from *Harter's Picture Archive*, edited by Jim Harter
(1978); and from *Picture Sourcebook for Collage and Decoupage*, edited by Edmund V. Gillon, Jr.
(1974); all published by Dover Publications, Inc.

Contents

How to Use this Book 1

Introduction: The Construction of Láadan 3

The Sounds of Láadan 7

GRAMMAR
Lesson 1 9
Lesson 2 13
Lesson 3 17
Lesson 4 21
Lesson 5 25
Lesson 6 29
Lesson 7 33
Lesson 8 37
Lesson 9 41
Lesson 10 45
Lesson 11 49
Lesson 12 53
Lesson 13 57
Lesson 14 59

DICTIONARY
English to Láadan 61
Láadan to English 91

Rules of Grammar 129

Miscellaneous Additional Information
Days of the Week, Months of the Year,
    "Love Nouns", Numbers, Pronouns 135
Songs /Psalms 139
Lessons that originally appeared in *Hot Wire*) 147

Conclusion. 157

Publisher's Acknowledgements

This book was made possible through the efforts of many people whom I want to acknowledge and thank: Suzette Haden Elgin, of course, for the obvious: the inventing of Láadan, and the writing of this book; and also for the not-so-obvious: her support and encouragement as I undertook a project that grew to consume most of my spare time and energy for far longer than I believed possible. Richard S. Russell, my partner of many years, for the use of his computer and printer (and for his much-needed advice and assistance). Port-to-Print of Madison, WI, for transferring the data files from PC to Macintosh format, saving me many of hours of re-entry. Karen Robinson of Raleigh, NC, for her extensive work in compiling the Láadan-to-English Dictionary. Toni Armstrong, of Chicago, IL, for permission to reprint the lessons originally appearing in *Hot Wire* magazine. The many readers of the first edition, whose comments and interest kept Láadan alive and growing. And the members of SF³, for letting me convince them to sponsor this project.

Diane Martin
Madison, Wisconsin

Technical Production Notes: This book was produced on a Macintosh II computer using WriteNow, and an AST TurboLaser/PS printer. The primary typeface is New Century Schoolbook. The cover and interior stock are Nekoosa Textweave. Printed by Odana Press, of Madison, WI

Macintosh is a trademark of Apple Computer, Inc. WriteNow is a trademark licensed to T/Maker Co. TurboLaser is a registered trademark of AST research.

How To Use This Book

    Láadan is a language constructed by a woman, for women, for the specific purpose of expressing the perceptions of women. This grammar and dictionary are intended to introduce you to the language and give you an opportunity to see if it is of interest to you or could be useful to you. Each grammar unit has both a core section and a supplementary section that expands on the core. You might find it best to read through all the core sections first to get the feel and weight of the language, and then return to the supplementary sections.

    Vocabulary from the Grammar is listed in the Dictionary section, which is divided into an English-to-Láadan section and a (new to this edition) Láadan-to-English section; following the Dictionary is a set of miscellaneous information, additional vocabulary, and, for reference purposes, a brief listing of the basic rules of Láadan grammar.

Introduction:

The Construction of Láadan

In the fall of 1981, I was involved in several seemingly unrelated activities. I had been asked to write a scholarly review of the book *Women and Men Speaking*, by Cheris Kramarae; I was working on a speech for the WisCon science fiction convention scheduled for March 1982, where I was to be Guest of Honor; and I was reading—and re-reading—Douglas Hofstadter's *Göedel, Escher, Bach*. I had also been reading a series of papers by Cecil Brown and his associates on the subject of lexicalization—that is, the giving of names (words, in most cases, or parts of words) to units of meaning in human languages. Out of this serendipitous mix came a number of things.

(1) I became aware, through Kramarae's book, of the feminist hypothesis that existing human languages are inadequate to express the perceptions of women. This intrigued me because it had a built-in paradox: if it is true, the only mechanism available to women for discussing the problem is the very same language(s) alleged to be inadequate for the purpose.

(2) There occurred to me an interesting possibility within the framework of the Sapir-Whorf Hypothesis (briefly, that language structures perceptions): if women had a language adequate to express their perceptions, it might reflect a quite different reality than that perceived by men. This idea was reinforced for me by the papers of Brown *et al.*, in which there was constant reference to various phenomena of lexicalization as the only natural and self-evident possibilities. I kept thinking that women would have done it differently, and that what was being called the "natural" way to create words seemed to me to be instead the <u>male</u> way to create words.

(3) I read in *Göedel, Escher, Bach* a reformulation of Göedel's Theorem, in which Hofstadter proposed that for every record player there were records it could not play because they would lead to its indirect self-destruction. And it struck me that if you squared this you would get a hypothesis that for every language there were perceptions it could not express because they would lead to its indirect self-destruction. Furthermore, if you cubed it, you would get a hypothesis that for every culture there are languages it could not use because they would lead to its indirect self-destruction. This made me wonder: what would happen to American culture if women did have and did use a language that expressed their perceptions? Would it self-destruct?

(4) I focused my Guest of Honor speech for WisCon on the question of why women portraying new realities in science fiction had, so far as I knew, dealt only with Matriarchy and Androgyny, and never with the third alternative based on the hypothesis that women are not superior to men (Matriarchy) or interchangeable with and equal to men (Androgyny) but rather entirely different from men. I proposed that it was at least possible that this was because the only language available to women excluded the third reality. Either because it was unlexicalized and thus no words existed with which to write about it, or it was lexicalized in so cumbersome a manner that it was useless for the writing of fiction, or the lack of lexical resources literally made it impossible to imagine such a reality.

Somewhere along the way, this all fell together for me, and I found myself with a cognitive brew much too fascinating to ignore. The only question was how I was to go about exploring all of this. A scientific experiment and a scholarly monograph would have been nice; but I knew what the prospects of funding would be for an investigation of these matters, and I was without the private income that would have let me ignore that aspect of the problem. I therefore chose as medium the writing of a science fiction novel about a future America in which the woman-language had been constructed and was in use. That book, called *Native Tongue* was published by DAW Books in August 1984. Its sequel, *Native Tongue II: The Judas Rose,* appeared from DAW in February 1987.

In order to write the book, I felt obligated to at least try to construct the language. I'm not an engineer, and when I write about engines I make no attempt to pretend that I know how engines are put together or how they function. But I am a linguist, and knowing how languages work is supposed to be my home territory. I didn't feel that I could ethically just fake the woman-language, or just insert a handful of hypothetical words and phrases to represent it. I needed at least the basic grammar and a modest vocabulary, and I needed to experience what such a project would be <u>like</u>. I therefore began, on June 28, 1982, the construction of the language that became Láadan.

Because I am a linguist, I have studied many existing languages, from a number of different language families. In the construction of Láadan I have tried to use features of those languages which seemed to me to be valuable and appropriate. This method of construction is often called "patchwork", and is not looked upon with great favor in the Patriarchal Paradigm that dominates contemporary science. I would remind you, nonetheless, that among women the patchwork quilt is recognized as an artform, and the methodology of patchwork is respected.

My original goal was to reach a vocabulary of 1,000 words—enough, if well chosen, for ordinary conversation and informal writing. I passed that goal early on, and in the fall of 1982 the journal *Women and Language News* published the first writing in the language, a Nativity story written from Mary's point of view.

There was one more factor that entered into my decision to construct Láadan, and I saved it for last because it was not there originally but developed out of the work that I was doing. I found myself discussing the idea of the woman-language, proposed need for it, etc., at meetings and conferences and among my friends and colleagues. And I found that it was possible to get the necessary concepts across, if I was patient. (There was, for example, the useful fact that English has no word whatsoever for what a woman does during the sexual act...this generally helps to make some points more clear.) But I got thoroughly tired of one question and its answer. People would ask me, "Well, if existing human languages are inadequate to express women's perceptions, why haven't they ever made one up that is adequate?" And all I could ever say was that I didn't know.[1] This became tiresome, and frustrating, and it was a relief to me when I was at last able to say, "Well, as a matter of fact, a woman did construct such a language, beginning on June 28, 1982, and its name is Láadan."

This book is a teaching grammar of Láadan, with an accompanying

---

[1] At that time I had not yet had the opportunity to read Mary Daly's book, published in May 1984, called *Pure Lust*. In that book Daly tells us that St. Hildegarde of Bingen, who lived from 1098–1179, constructed a language consisting of 900 words, with an alphabet of 23 letters. She was a distinguished scholar, with publications to her credit in a number of fields; as Daly says, it is impossible for us to know how much of value was lost to us when this language was lost. And I now have an alternative answer to that persistent question, although I have no way of knowing whether St. Hildegarde's motivation for the construction of her language was a sense that no language adequate to express her perceptions was available to her.

dictionary. It is only a beginning, and for all I know, the beginning of a failure, something that will never be of interest to anyone but the collector of linguistic exotica. But because this book exists, it will be very hard to "lose" Láadan in the way that other languages have been swallowed up by the History of Mankind. For that, I am most grateful to the members of SF^3, who thought the work was important enough to justify publication.

Suzette Haden Elgin
near Old Alabam, Arkansas

The Sounds
of Láadan

Láadan was constructed to be simple to pronounce. This description is tailored for speakers of English, because the material is written in English; but the sound system has been designed to present as few difficulties as possible, no matter what the native language of the learner.

Vowels: a   as in "c<u>a</u>lm"
                 e   as in "b<u>e</u>ll"
                 i   as in "b<u>i</u>t"
                 o   as in "h<u>o</u>me"
                 u   as in "d<u>u</u>ne"

Consonants: **b, d, sh, m, n, l, r, w, y, h** — as in English

              th   as in "<u>th</u>ink"
              zh   as in "plea<u>s</u>ure"

There is one more consonant in Láadan; it is "*lh*" and it has no English equivalent. If you put the tip of your tongue firmly against the roof of your mouth at the point where it begins to arch upward, draw the corners of your lips back as you would for an exaggerated smile, and try to say English "sh", the result should be an adequate "*lh* ". It is a sound with a hissing quality, and is not especially pleasant to hear. In Láadan it occurs only in words that are themselves references to something unpleasant, and can be added to words to give them a negative meaning. This is patterned after a similar feature of Navajo, and is something so very handy that I have always wished it existed in English

When a Láadan vowel is written with an accent mark above it, it is a vowel with high tone. English doesn't have any tones, but that will be no problem for you, since you can express it as heavy stress. Think of the way that you distinguish the noun "convert" from the verb "convert" by stressing one of the two syllables. If you pronounce a high-toned Láadan vowel as you would pronounce a strongly-stressed English syllable, you will achieve the same effect as high tone. Because Láadan does not use English stress, this will not be a source of confusion.

Lesson 1

PATTERN:

[Verb (Negative) Case Phrase—Subject]

(NOTE: Don't be concerned about the notation above; it will be useful in the long run. A "Case Phrase" is the same thing as what traditional English grammars call a "prepositional phrase." In English this means a preposition and its following noun phrase, as in "with a hatchet" or "to the beach", most of the time; in Láadan it usually means a noun phrase and its ending. This will become clear as we go along, and each of the sentence patterns explained will use the notation, with "Case Phrase" abbreviated to just "CP" in future to save space. "Case Phrase—Subject" will be written "CP-S." The parentheses around "Negative" mean that it is an optional element in the sentence.)

Vocabulary:

Bíi	(declarative)
ra	(no, not, negative)
i	(and)
izh	(but)
be	(she, he, it)
bezh	(they, few)
ben	(they, many)
ro	(weather)
with	(woman, person)
wa	(SEE NOTE BELOW)
thal	(to be good)
hal	(to work)

Examples:
   (a) Bíi thal ro wa.
>   The weather's good.
   (b) Bíi thal ra ro wa.
>   The weather's not good.

NOTE: A Láadan sentence begins with a word that tells you what sort of sentence it is—statement, question, request, etc. The most common of the words is "*Bíi*," which begins declarative sentences, ordinary statements. A Láadan sentence ends with a word that states why the speaker considers the sentence to be true; in the example it is "*wa*," which means "claimed to be true because the speaker herself perceived whatever has been said". "*Wa*" is probably the most common of these words, which are called "Evidence Morphemes".
   (c) Bíi hal with wa.
>   The woman works.
   Bíi hal ra with wa.
>   The woman doesn't work.

   (d) Bíi hal be wa.
>   She works.
   Bíi mehal bezh wa.
>   They work.(2 to 5 persons)
   Bíi mehal ben wa.
>   They work. (more than 5 persons)

   (e) Bíi hal with wa.
>   The woman works.
   Bíi mehal with wa.
>   The women work.

Rules:
   1. The basic sentence begins with a Speech Act Morpheme to indicate what the sentence does, and ends with an Evidence Morpheme. (When several sentences are used together by one person, and these remain the same, they don't have to be put on every single sentence—this will become clear.)
   2. The verb comes before the noun phrase in Láadan.
   3. To make a sentence negative, just put "*ra*" immediately after the verb.

4. To make a verb plural, put the prefix "*me-*" at the beginning of the word. (Notice that the shape of the noun phrase doesn't change in the plural.)

5. Láadan doesn't divide adjectives and verbs into two classes as English does. Thus "*thal*" means "be good" without any need for a separate word "be" in the sentence.

SUPPLEMENTAL SECTION:

1. Bíi hal   omid   wa.   HORSE
               háawith   CHILD
               omá   TEACHER
               thul   PARENT
               ábedá   FARMER

     The _____ works.
NOTICE: Láadan has no separate words for "a" or "the".

2. Bíi hal ra áwith   wa.   BABY
               rul   CAT
               mahina   FLOWER
               ezha   SNAKE

     The _____ doesn't work.

3. Bíi   áya   be   wa.   BEAUTIFUL
               balin   OLD
               lawida   PREGNANT
               wam   STILL, BUSY
               shóod   BUSY
               lath   CELIBATE BY CHOICE

     She is _____ .

4. Bíi   amedara be wa.   DANCES
               yod   EATS
               ada   LAUGHS
               ma   LISTENS
               osháana   MENSTRUATES
               wéedan   READS
               wod   SITS
               rúu   LIES DOWN

     She _____.

NOTE: For this (and all the other) supplementary sections, it would be good if you would practice combining the patterns you know—make the positive sentences negative by adding "ra", make the singular verbs plural by adding "*me-*" and so on. Láadan is a language that works to maintain a pattern of alternating consonants and vowels, for ease of pronunciation; for this reason, you can't put "*me-*" directly on a verb that begins with a vowel. In such a case, you insert an "*h*" to keep the pattern. Here are a few examples:

Bíi hal ra omid wa.	The horse doesn't work.
Bíi mehal ra omid wa.	The horses don't work.
Bíi áya mahina wa.	The flower is beautiful.
Bíi meháya mahina wa.	The flowers are beautiful.
Bíi mehada ben wa.	They laugh.

Lesson 2

PATTERN:

[(Auxiliary) Verb (NEG) CP–S]

Vocabulary:

Báa	(question)
eril	(PAST)
aril	(FUTURE)
le	(I)
ne	(you, one)
em	(yes)
mid	(creature, any animal
dala	(plant, any growing thing)
wíi	(to be alive)
owa	(to be warm)
híya	(to be small)
óoha	(to be weary)

Examples:

(a) Bíi eril wíi mid wa.
　　　The creature was alive.
　　Bíi eril wíi ra mid wa.
　　　The creature wasn't alive.

(b) Bíi aril mehóoha with wa.
　　　The women will be weary.
　　Bíi eril mehóoha with wa.
　　　The women were weary.

(c) Bíi híya dala waɛ.
> The plant is small.

Báa híya dala?
> Is the plant small?

(d) Báa owa ne?
> Are you warm?

=Em, owa le wa.
> =Yes, I'm warm.

=Ra, owa ra le wa.
> =No, I'm not warm.

Rules:

1. When you need to indicate time in a sentence, put an auxiliary immediately before the verb. Auxiliaries never change their shape in any way, even if the verb itself is made plural.

2. When you ask a question, you aren't providing information but are asking for some. Therefore, you don't need an Evidence Morpheme at the end of a question.

NOTE: If you speak English, you may find all these remarks about parts of the sentence being optional, only being used if needed, etc., very confusing—or annoying. Please don't be concerned. If you prefer, use as your rule that you will always put a Speech Act morpheme at the beginning of your sentence, or that you will always use an auxiliary to make your sentence time clear. The result may be very formal Láadan, but it will be grammatical.

SUPPLEMENTAL SECTION:

1. Báa eril

wóoban ne?	GIVE BIRTH
mime	ASK
lothel	KNOW
bedi	LEARN
benem	STAY
ulanin	STUDY
om	TEACH

Did you_____?

(Remember that the plural of *"ulanin"* will be *"mehulanin"* and the plural of *"om"* will be *"mehom"*. So, *"Báa eril mehom nen?"* is the sentence for asking a group of people "Did you teach?")

2. Báa eril   sholan be?   ALONE
              loyo   BLACK
              leyan   BROWN
              aba   FRAGRANT
              liyen   GREEN
              sho   HEAVY

         Was it _____ *?*

3. Báa   eril   hal ne?   *PAST:* Did you work?
           aril   *FUTURE:* Will you work?
           ril   *PRESENT:* Are you working (now)?
           eríli   *FAR PAST:* Did you work long ago?
           aríli   *FAR FUTURE:* Will you work sometime far ahead?
           rilrili   *HYPOTHETICAL:* Would you work?
                                     Might you work?
                                     Let's suppose you worked...

Lesson 3

PATTERN:

[(Aux) Verb (Neg) CP–S CP–Object]

Vocabulary:

rana	(drink)
ana	(food)
áana	(sleep)
nezh	(you, few)
nen	(you, many)
-(e)th	(OBJECT ending
néde	(to want)
den	(to help)
di	(to say, speak)
wi	(EVIDENCE MORPHEME) "Wi" means "self-evident to everyone".

Examples:

(a) Bíi owa ana wa.
   The food is hot. (said because the speaker perceives it)

   Bíi owa ana wi.
   The food is hot. (said because it is obvious to everyone)

(b) Bíi aril néde with áanath wa.
   The woman will want sleep.

   Bíi eril menéde with anath wa.
   The women didn't want food.

17

(c) Bíi eril den with neneth wa.
       The woman helped you.
Bíi eril den be witheth wa.
       She helped the woman.

(d) Bíi aril di le Láadan wa.
       I will speak Láadan.

NOTE: Example (d) is a good illustration of what is meant by "if you need it." It would not be ungrammatical to put an object ending on the word Láadan and say "*Bíi aril di le Láadaneth*". But it is impossible for a language to speak a person, and the subject always comes before the object in Láadan sentences. This means that the object ending is not really needed and can be left off, and it is more natural to do so. Also, just as Láadan allows two vowels together only if one of them is a high-toned vowel, it does not allow two consonants together in most cases. (Although "*th, sh, zh, lh*" are written as two consonants, each of them is only one consonant sound—like English "sh, ch".) If you added the object ending "-*th*" to "*Láadan*" or to "*nen*" you would break that rule—the "e" is inserted to keep that from happening.

(e) Bíi eril di		be	Láadan wa.	
				She spoke Láadan.
	ndi	bezh		
				They (few) spoke Láadan.
	ndi (or nedi) ben			
				They (many) spoke Láadan.

Rules:
    1. To mark a Case Phrase as an object, add "-*th*"; if the word ends in a consonant, use "-*eth*". NOTICE that there is no ending for the Case Phrase that is a subject.
    2. When a verb begins with "*d*", the plural prefix is "*n*". This is what is known as a "syllabic *n*", and English has syllabic "*n*" at the end of words like "button". Speakers that find the syllabic "*n*" uncomfortable often use "*ne-*", and that is perfectly all right; it is just less formal. (There are no other rules for making verbs plural.)

SUPPLEMENTAL SECTION:

1. Bíi eril néde le esheth wa.   BOAT, esh
                         áabeth   BOOK, áabe
                         yobeth   COFFEE, yob
                         losheth   MONEY, losh
                         lotheth   INFORMATION, loth

      I wanted _____.

2. Bíi eril yod be baleth wa.   BREAD, bal
                         ódoneth   CHEESE, odon
                         thilith   FISH, thili
                         yuth   FRUIT, yu
                         medath   VEGETABLE, meda
                         anadaleth (a) MEAL, anadal

      She ate _____.

3. Báa aril meden with   áwitheth?   BABY, áwith
                        obetheth   NEIGHBOR, obeth
                       babíth   BIRD, babí
                       romideth   WILD ANIMAL, romid
                       shamideth DOMESTIC ANIMAL, shamid
                       bediháth   STUDENT, bedihá
                       eháth   SCIENTIST, ehá

      Will the women help the _____?

19

Lesson 4

PATTERN:

[(Aux) Verb Complex (Neg) CP–S]

Vocabulary:

balin	(old)
áya	(beautiful)
wáa	(EVIDENCE MORPHEME)
wo-	(a prefix; explained below)

NOTE: When "*wáa*" is used, the speaker is stating that the source of the information is one she trusts, even though she has no personal perception of that information to rely on.

Examples:
(a) Bíi néde hal with wáa.
    The woman wants to work.
Bíi eril néde hal with wáa.
    The woman wanted to work.
Bíi eril mende mehal with wáa.
    The women wanted to work.

(b) Bíi néde hal ra with wáa.
    The woman didn't want to work.

(c) Bíi balin with wáa.
   The woman is old.
Bíi aya with wáa.
   The woman is beautiful.
Bíi aya wobalin wowith wáa.
   The old woman is beautiful.
Bíi meháa mewobalin wowith wáa.
   The old women are beautiful.

(d) Bíi néde hal wobalin wowith wáa.
   The old woman wants to work.
Bíi néde al ra wobalin wowith wáa.
   The old woman doesn't want to work.

Rules:
1. The sequence: "to want + to VERB" in Láadan forms a single unit called a Verb Complex, which is used just like an ordinary verb. The auxiliary goes before it, the negative follows it, and nothing can go between its two parts. Since two verbs are used, both must be marked plural if either is. As always, the auxiliary does not change its form.
2. Láadan has a form that is much like an English adjective + noun sequence, as in "green tree" or "small child". You can take any sequence of verb and subject (remembering that "adjectives" are only ordinary verbs in Láadan) and put the marker "wo-" at the beginning of each one. "Beautiful woman" is thus "wohaya wowith". This is very useful, but it is a bit different from English, because it can only be used if you have just one verb. You cannot use this pattern to translate an English sequence like "little red brick wall".
3. The plural marker is always the first piece in any verb; thus "beautiful women" will be "mewoháya wowith".
4. You will have no trouble with combining the parts of the words in these patterns if you just add the endings before you add "wo-". So, "I helped the woman" is "Bíi eril den le withéeth wa"; "I helped the weary woman" is "Bíi eril den le wohóoya wowitheth". You would not put an object marker on a verb, you see.

SUPPLEMENTAL SECTION:

1. Bíi eril yod be   worúsho   wohanath wa.   BITTER, rúsho
                     wohéeda   SACRED, héeda
                     womáanan   SALTY, máanan
                     woméenan   SWEET, méenan

   She ate the _____ food.
   (yod = eat; wo+ana (food) + object ending = wohanath)

   NOTE: "*Wa*" is used in the example, meaning that the speaker knows from her personal perception that the food is bitter, salty, etc. If she knows that only because she has been told that it is so and trusts the source, she will use "*wáa*" instead. If everyone present can obviously see or otherwise perceive the characteristic of the food, she may use "*wi*".

2. Bíi néde le   worahíya woháabeth wa.   BIG, rahíya
                 woleyi   BLUE, leyi
                 woleyan   BROWN, leyan
                 wolula   PURPLE, lula
                 wolaya   RED, laya
                 wolíithi   WHITE, líithi
                 woleli   YELLOW, leli

   I want the _____ book. (áabe = book)

3. Báa néde   lith   withid?   THINK
              lothel   KNOW
              en   UNDERSTAND
              dom   REMEMBER
              wéedan   READ
              thod   WRITE
              lishid   SIGN (as in sign language)
   Does the man want to _____ ?

   NOTE: The masculine ending is "*-id*", so that if it is necessary to specify that a person is male, you can do so by adding "*-id*" to the basic form. Here "*with+id*" means "man".

23

Lesson 5

PATTERN:

[(Aux) Verb (Neg) CP–S (CP–O) CP–GOAL]

Vocabulary:

wida	(to carry)	lezh, len	(we-few, we-many)
sháad	(to come, to go)	nezh, nen	(you-few, you-many)
ban	(to give)	-di	(GOAL ending)
beth	(home)	du-	(try to VERB)
weth	(way, road)		

NOTE: The verb prefix "*du-*" is very useful. You have the verb "*wida*", meaning "to carry"; make it "*duwida*" and you have "try to carry". As always, the plural marker comes first; thus, if many people are involved in the act, the word is "*meduwida*".

Examples:

(a) Bíi aril sháad le bethedi wa.
　　　　I will go home.
　Bíi aril mesháad lezh bethedi wa.
　　　　We (few) will go home.
　Bíi aril mesháad len bethedi wa.
　　　　We (many) will go home.

(b) Bíi aril sháad le wethedi wa.
　　　　I'll go to the road.
　Bíi ari dusháad le wethedi wa.
　　　　I'll try to go to the road.

25

(c) Bíi eril wida le ənath wethedi wa.
   I carried the food to the road.

(d) Báa eril ban ne anath withedi?
   Did you give the food to the woman?

Rules:
   1. To mark a Case Phrase as a Goal, use the ending "-*di*". As always, if the word ends in a consonant, use "-*edi*".
   2. You may not be used to talking about the "case" of noun phrases. Case is the term that refers to the role the noun phrase has in a sentence—that is, whether it is something that acts, something acted upon, something used to act, etc. The three cases we have used so far are Subject, Object, and Goal; a Goal Case Phrase is the one to which or toward which something is directed. (A Case Phrase is just a noun phrase plus its case-marker ending; a noun phrase is any sequence that can fill a case role, such as a noun or a pronoun.)

SUPPLEMENTAL SECTION:

1. Bíi eril ban le beth oninedi   wa.   NURSE, onin
                          hudi   BOSS, hu
                          ebadi   SPOUSE, eba
                          háawithedi   CHILD, háawith
                          zhilhadedi   PRISONER, zhilhad
                          haládi   WORKER, halá
                          duthahádi   HEALER, duthahá
                          lanemidedi   DOG, lanemid

I gave it to the _____ . *(be + th = it, Object)*

NOTE: The suffix (ending) "-*a*" is like English "-er, -ist". You see it here in "worker". You can use this piece to form many words from verbs. It is worth looking at the word for "healer" in the example. "To heal" is "*dutha*"; to add "-*á*" you must insert an "*h*" even though a sequence of two vowels is allowed when one of them is high-toned, because the second vowel is a meaningful piece (a morpheme) all by itself.

2. Báa eril sháad ne

hozhazhedi	AIRPORT, hohazh
oódóodi	BRIDGE, oódóo
áathamedi	CHURCH, áatham
shéedi	DESERT, shée
ábededi	FARM, ábed
olinedi	FOREST, olin
bothedi	HOTEL, both
maridi	ISLAND, mari
belidedi	HOUSE, belid
hothedi	PLACE, hoth
mewithedi	TOWN/CITY, mewith

Did you go to the _____ ?

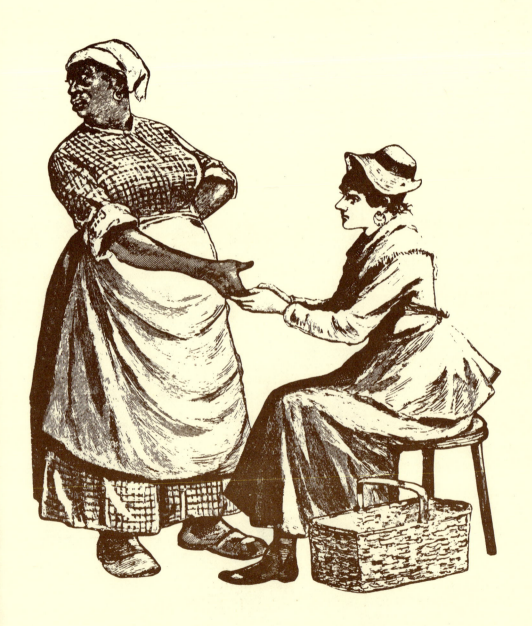

28

Lesson 6

PATTERN:

    [(Aux) Verb (Neg) CP–S (CP–O) CP–SOURCE]

Vocabulary:

bel	(take)	thel	(get)
dan	(language)	-de	SOURCE ending
edaná	(linguist)	ná-	continue to VERB,
menedebe	(many)		keep VERBing

Examples:

(a) Bíi eril sháad le wethede wa.
        I came from the road.
   Bíi eril mesháad with wethede wa
        The women come from the road.

(b) Bíi eril sháad ben wethede.
        They came from the road.
   Bíi eril násháad ben wethede.
        They kept coming from the road.

(c) Bíi eril bel le anath edanáde wa
        I took the food from the linguist.
   Bíi eril bel le anath edanáde menedebe wa.
        I took the food from the many linguists.

(d) Bíi eril thel le anath withede i edanáde wa.
        I got the food from the woman and the linguist.

NOTE: The two examples in (b) above do not have any Evidence Morpheme at the end, and they are not in a series of connected sentences that would indicate what the speaker intended. This is possible in Láadan, but it can mean only one thing: that the speaker does not wish to state the reason why she considers what she says to be true.

Rules:
1. To mark a Case Phrase as a Source, use the ending "*-de*". If the word ends in a consonant, you'll need to use "*-ede*", of course.
2. There are times when you néed to indicate a plural, but you have no verb to take the plural marker, as in the second sentence of (c) above. You can then put the word "*menedebe*" ("many") immediately after the noun phrase you want to make plural. The same thing is done with numbers, and with the words "*nedebe*", meaning "few, several" and "*woho*" meaning "all, every". These words never change their form, never add prefixes or suffixes; thus, if those "many linguists" up there were Object Case Phrase members you would use "*edanáth menedebe*". The case marker would never appear on "*menedebe*".
3. You will notice that a sentence such as "*Bíi eril sháad le wethedi wa*", meaning "I went to the road" is exactly like "*Bíi eril sháad le wethede wa*", meaning "I came from the road". You can only tell the direction of the motion verb by the case ending on "road". Speakers of some languages are not comfortable keeping the vowels "*i*" and "*e*" separate, because in their languages they are only one sound. In such a situation, and if no other information is available in the sentence to make things clear, it is correct to use "*-dim*" as an alternate form for the Goal Case Phrase. Such a speaker could say "*Bíi eril sháad le wethidim wa*" for "I went to the house".

BRIEF READING
Bíi eril methi[1] with menedebe dosheth[2] wa. Medi with, "Bíi methi ra len daneth wa. Methi withed daneth, izh len—ra. Menéde medi len, izh methi ra len dáaneth[3] menedebe. Menáde medi, izh methad[4] len ra." Id[5] medi edaná, "Bíi aril meden len neneth wa."

[1] thi	= to have
[2] dosh	= burden
[3] dáan	= word
[4] thad	= to be able
[5] id	= and then

Free Translation:

There were many women who had a burden. The women said, "We have no language. Men have a language, but as for us—no. We want to speak, but there are many words we don't have. We want to speak, but we can't." And then the linguists said, "We will help you."

Notes on the Reading:

Notice that once the speaker has established that she is offering declarative sentences and is speaking on the basis of her own perception—by beginning with "*Bíi*" and ending with "*wa*" in her very first sentence—she does not have to keep doing that. If there were a change, if she wanted to ask a question or to offer information based on her trust in a source or something other than her perceptions, she would have to add the words that specify those things. Otherwise, listeners will assume that there is no change. The same thing holds for the auxiliary "*eril*" that indicates past time; it does not have to go into every sentence in a connected sequence. However, if you are not sure whether to use any of these sentence pieces, you will always be safe putting one in.

SUPPLEMENTAL SECTION:

1. Bíi eril bedi le Láadan lanede wa.   FRIEND, lan
                      omáde   TEACHER, omá
                      lebede   ENEMY, leb

   I learned Láadan from a/the _____ .

2. Báa eril mesháad nen wéehothede ?   LIBRARY, wéehoth
                          bode   MOUNTAIN, bo
                          melade   OCEAN, mela
                          wilide   RIVER/CREEK, wili
                          ulinede   SCHOOL, ulin
                          yedede   VALLEY, yed

   Did you come from the _____?

Lesson 7

PATTERN:
    [(Aux) Verb (Neg) CP–S (CP–O) CP–INSTRUMENT)]

Vocabulary:

oya	(skin)	thena	(joy)
oyu	(ear)	ilhi	(disgust)
oyi	(eye)	el	(to make)
oma	(hand)	láad	(to perceive)
ili	(water)	lolaád	(to perceive internally)
zho	(sound)	thad	(to be able)
		-nan	(INSTRUMENT ending)

Examples:
    (a) Bíi el le beth omanan wa.
                I make it with (my) hands.

    (b) Bíi láad le neth oyinan wa.   I see you.
       Bíi láad le neth oyunan wa.   I hear you.
       Bíi láad le zhoth oyunan wa.   I hear a sound.
       Bíi láad le ilith oyanan wa.   I feel the water.

    (c) Bíi eril loláad with thenath wáa.
                The woman was joyful.
    Bíi eril loláad with ilhith wáa.
                The woman was disgusted.

Rules and Explanation:

1. To mark a Case Phrase as an Instrument (as that which is used to do something), use the ending "*-nan*". Insert an "*e*" if necessary.

2. Láadan handles perceptions and emotions rather differently than English does. In Láadan you perceive things externally, with your eyes or your ears or your nose or your skin. Emotions are something you perceive internally, inside yourself. The first sentence in (b) says that the speaker perceives "you" and that the speakers' eyes are the instrument for that perception. We could translate it as "I see you with my eyes" in English, but that is a little superfluous—English "see" includes the information that it is done with eyes. In Láadan you could add an Instrumental Case Phrase to the examples in (d), using "with (my) mind" or "with (my) heart" or something of the kind, but it would be considered as odd as saying "I hear you with my ears" in English; the organ or organs of internal perception are assumed.

3. You could translate the examples in (c) as "The woman felt joy" and "The woman felt disgust" if you preferred, or if that phrasing seemed better in the context of your sentence.

4. In Láadan there are a number of different forms for the names of emotions, rather than a single word "joy" or "love" or "hate" and so on. The word translated as "joy" here is the most neutral form, meaning "joy for good reasons".

5. Finally, the object marker has been used in all the example sentences, and it is correct. But it is far more common to omit the object suffix on emotions (since love or disgust cannot "perceive" living things); similarly, it is much more common to say "*Bíi láad le zho oyunan wa*," than to use "*Zhoth*"; a sound cannot "hear" anything. This is a matter of personal choice and style, so long as the meaning cannot be misunderstood.

BRIEF READING:

Bíide[1] eril meloláad with menedebe shalath[2] wáa. Eril methi ra ben daneth. Id mesháad edaná i medi benedi, "Bre[3] menéde nen daneth, ébre aril mehel len daneth wa." Medi with, "Báa methad nen?" I medi edaná benedi, "Bíi aril dumethad wa." Eril meláad with beneth oyunan i menahul[4] ben wáa.

[1] bíide	=	I say in narrative, as in telling a story
[2] shala	=	grief for good reasons
[3] bre...ébre	=	if...then
[4] hul	=	hope; this form is the verb stem "*hul*" plus the prefix *na-* which means "to begin to VERB" plus the plural prefix

Free Translation:
Once there were many women who felt grief, and for good reasons. They had no language. And then the linguists came and said to them, "If you want a language, then we will make a language". The women said, "Can you do that?" And the linguists said to them, "We will try". The women heard them and began to hope.

Notes on the Reading:
In this example the speaker has established that she is telling a story by adding "-*de*" as the Speech Act morpheme at the very beginning. If it were a completely imaginary story, she would close her sentence with "*wo*", the hypothetical Evidence Morpheme; by using "*wáa*" instead, she is telling the listener that this is a story she considers to be true because she trusts the source of it. There is a whole set of other endings for "*Bíi*" to indicate the speaker's feelings, by the way; here are examples using the other ones:

Bíid = speaking in anger
Bíith = speaking in pain
Bíili = speaking in love
Bíilan = speaking in celebration
Bíida = speaking in jest, as a joke
Bíidi = speaking as a teacher
Bíiya = speaking in fear

SUPPLEMENTAL SECTION:

1. Bíi eril láad le   lalith   oyanan wa.   RAIN, lali
                            hisheth   SNOW, hish
                            rosheth   SUN, rosh
                            yuleth   WIND, yul

I felt the _____ .
(The object endings are optional here.)

2. Báa eril láad ne nith   oyinan?   CUP, ni
                          bodeth   DISH, bod
                          onidath   FAMILY
                          shidath   GAME
                          déelath   GARDEN
                          binith   GIFT
                          shenihaleth   COMPUTER, shenihal

Did you see the _____?

(Notice there's no need for me to write out the basic form for words like *"onidath"*; the *"a"* has to be part of the base word, because only *"e"* is inserted before endings.)

3. Bíi eril láad ra le zhazheth   oyunan wa.   AIRPLANE, zhazh
                   ohamedith   PRAYER
                   deleth   RADIO, del
                   dedideth   STORY, dedide
                   loroloth   THUNDER
                   ditheth   VOICE, dith
                   limlimeth   BELL, limlim

    I didn't hear the _____.

4. Bíi eril loláad with   am   wá.   LOVE, for one related by blood
                   sham   LOVE, for a child of her body
                   ad   LOVE, for one respected but not liked
                   ab   LOVE, for one liked but not respected
                   bala   ANGER, for good and not futile reasons
                   maha   SEXUAL DESIRE
                   heyi   PAIN
                   lash   INDIFFERENCE
                   shara   GRIEF, for good reasons, but futilely; that is,
                                       nothing can be done

    The woman felt _____.

36

Lesson 8

PATTERN:

$$\left[(\text{Aux}) \ \text{Verb} \ (\text{Neg}) \ \text{CP–S} \ \left\{\begin{array}{l}\text{CP–ASSOCIATE} \\ \text{CP–BENEFICIARY}\end{array}\right\}\right]$$

Vocabulary:

Wil sha	(Hello, Greetings)
Aala	(thank you)
Dóo	(Well...)
Bóo	(request, polite command)
-da	(BENEFICIARY ending)
-den	(ASSOCIATE ending, neutral)
-dan	(ASSOCIATE ending, with pleasure)

Examples:

(a) Bíi aril hal be witheden wáa.
　　　　　　　She'll work with the woman.
Bíi aril hal be withedan wáa.
　　　　　　　She'll work with the woman with pleasure.

(b) Bíi hal be witheda wa.
　　　　　　　She works for the woman.
Bíi hal be wobalin wowitheda wa.
　　　　　　　She works for the old woman.

(c) Bíi eril el le anath witheda wa.
　　　　　　　I made food for the woman.

Rules:

(1) To mark a Case Phrase as a Beneficiary (that for whom, or on whose behalf, something is done), add the ending "-*da*".

(2) To mark a Case Phrase as an Associate (with whom something is done, as in English "I danced with her"), add the ending "-*den*". If you want to indicate that there is pleasure in the association you may use the alternative Associate marker "-*dan*"; "-*den*" is a neutral form.

(3) The Beneficiary marker given above is the one used when something is done voluntarily. There are three alternative forms:

- *-dá*   against one's will when forced or coerced
- *-daá*   accidentally
- *-dáa*   not because of force or coercion, but because of an obligation of law or duty that one accepts.

In any other situation, use "-*da*".

BRIEF READING:

Bíide eril láad with háawitheth[1] oyinan wo. Eril delishe[2] háawith. Di with, "Wil sha, háawith! Bóo delishe ra ne!" Izh nádelishe háawith. Eril di with, "Báa loláad ne heyi?" "Ra," di háawith. "Bíi loláad ra le heyi wa. Delishe le bróo[3] aril di rawith[4] leden." Di with, "Dóo, ril[5] di le neden. Ril di le neden i nedan wa." I di háawith withedi, "Aála!" I eril nodelishe[6] háawith wáa.

[1] háawith	=	child
[2] delishe	=	to cry, to weep
[3] bróo	=	because
[4] rawith	=	nobody
[5] ril	=	now
[6] nodelishe	=	stop + to cry

Free Translation:

Once a woman saw a child. The child was crying. The woman said, "Hello, child! Please don't cry!" But the child kept crying. The woman said, "Do you hurt? Do you feel pain somewhere?" "No," said the child. "I don't hurt. I cry because nobody will talk with me." The woman said, "Well, I am talking with you right now. I am talking with you and I do so with pleasure." And the child said to the woman, "Thank you!" And the child stopped crying.

SUPPLEMENTAL SECTION:

1. Bóo aril   lo   leden.   REJOICE
                 edethi   SHARE
                 lishid   SIGN
                 alehala   MUSIC (that is, make music)
                 amedara   DANCE (Notice that no Evidence Morpheme is used after "Bóo".)

Please _____ with me. or *Would you _____ with me?*

2. Bíi néde le   dizheth   laneda wa.   KETTLE, dizh
                     dínídineth   TOY, dínídin
                     bineth   BOWL, bin
                     idoneth   BRUSH, idon
                     doneth   COMB, don
                     odeth   CLOTH, od
                     oweth   GARMENT, owe
                     dimilineth   ORNAMENT, dimilin

I want a/the _____ for a friend.

3. Bíi eril   eb   le beth laneda wa.   BUY
                ri   RECORD
                nori   SEND
                redeb   FIND
                déedan   INTERPRET
                héedan   TRANSLATE

I _____ it for a friend. (all in past tense)

NOTE: the verb "*lishid*," which means "to sign" as in a sign language, may have added to it the same set of endings that are allowed with the Speech Act morphemes like "*Bíi*". This is also true for the verb "*dama*," which means "to touch."

Lesson 9

PATTERN:

$$\left[\text{(Aux) Verb (Neg) CP–S} \left\{ \begin{array}{c} \text{CP–Time} \\ \text{CP–Place} \end{array} \right\} \right]$$

Vocabulary:

Aril	(Goodbye)	náal	(night)
e...e	(either...or)	-ya	(TIME ending)
o	(around)	-ha	(PLACE ending)
obée	(during)		

Examples:

    (a) Bíi aril mesháad ben bethedi náaleya wáa.
        They will go home at night.

    (b) Bíi eril mehal ben betheha wáa.
        They worked at home.

    (c) Bíi hal le betheha o wa.
        I work around home.

    (d) Bíi hal le náaleya obée wa.
        I work during the night.

    (e) Bíi aril hal e with e withid wáa.
        Either the woman or the man will work.

Rules and Explanation:

    (1) To mark a Case Phrase as Time, add the ending "*-ya*".

    (2) To mark a Case Phrase as Place, add the ending "*-ha*".

    (3) These two endings specify an event or state as being at a particular location in space or time. English has a wide variety of prepositions which are used in such CP's to make the information more precise; thus, something will

41

be said to be not just "at" a particular location but "inside, between, underneath, before", and so on. In English these prepositions are used as the first element in the phrase and could be said to be used instead of a more general case-marking preposition. In Láadan the general marker is always used, but there is a set of more narrow forms that can be added to the phrase to make its meaning more precise. We can say that "-ya" and ha" mean "at" some time or place; if more precise information is required, the speaker puts an additional locational word at the end of the Case Phrase as in example (d) above. "Bíi hal le náaleya wa" is gramatical and means "I work at night"; "Bíi hal le náaleya obée wa" adds "during" to the sentence at the speaker's option. The set of words like "obée" (called postpositions) is made up of words which never change their form in any way; they take no affixes at all.

BRIEF READING:

Bíide erili násháad Dumidu[1] wethaha wo . Eril láad be éelen[2] oyinan. Lith be, "Womemeénan wohéelen!" Eril nahoób[3], be; duthel be éeleneth. Izh eril dúuthel[4] be beneth. Eril mehíthihal[5] éelen. Id eril di Dumidul, "Dóo, néde ra le éelheneth! Néde ra rawith éelheneth! Bíi meyemehul[6] éelen wa!"

[1] dumidu	= fox	
[2] éelen	= grape(s)	
[3] oób	= to jump	
[4] dúu	= try in vain to VERB; it is a prefix	
[5] mehíthihal	= to be very high	
[6] meyemehul	= to be extremely sour	

Free Translation:

Once, a very long time ago, a fox was going along a road. He saw some grapes. He thought, "Sweet-tasting grapes!" He started jumping; he tried to get the grapes. But he tried in vain to get them. The grapes were very high. And then the Fox said, "Well, I don't want the darned grapes! Nobody wants those old grapes! I can tell that they're horribly sour!"

Notes on the Translation:

In this reading you see the use of the Láadan sound "lh" to add a negative meaning. The Fox calls the grapes "éelen" as long as he has only positive feelings about them. But when he becomes upset because he can't reach them, he calls them "*éelhen*", translated here as "darned grapes" and "those old grapes". You can always, in Láadan, change an "*l*" to "*lh*" or add a "*lh*" to a word to give it a negative meaning. And of course, the Fox is deliberately lying in this story. Notice that in the last sentence he uses "*wa*" as his Evidence Morpheme, indicating that he claims the grapes are horribly sour because he has personally perceived them to be so—this has been translated as "I can tell..." The reader is able to determine from the context that the Fox is making this up.

SUPPLEMENTAL SECTION:

(1) Bíi hal with

loshebelideya wa.	BANK, loshebelid
shodeya	ROOM, shod
duneya	FIELD, dun
áatheya	DOOR, áath
sheniya	INTERSECTION, sheni
weheya	STORE, wehe
duthahotheya	HOSPITAL, duthahoth
sheshihotheya	BEACH, sheshihoth

The woman works at/in the _____.

(2) Báa hal na

sháaleha	?	DAY, sháal
Henesháaleha		MONDAY, Henesháal
Aleleha		JANUARY, Alel
wemeneha		SPRING, wemen
wumaneha		SUMMER, wuman
díidineha		HOLIDAY, díidin

Do you work on/in _____?

43

Lesson 10

PATTERN:

$$\left[\text{(Aux) Verb (Neg) CP–S} \left\{ \begin{array}{l} \text{CP–IDENTIFIER} \\ \text{CP–MANNER} \\ \text{CP–CAUSE} \end{array} \right\} \right]$$

Vocabulary:

lothel	(to know, not said of people)
an	(to know, of people)
lóolo	(to be slow)
héeya	(to fear)
-nal	(MANNER ending)
-wan	(CAUSE ending
-wáan	(CAUSE ending
-∅	(IDENTIFIER ending)

Examples:

(a) Bíi le with wa.
   I am a woman.
Bíi le wothal wowith wa.
   I am a good woman.

(b) Bíi eril hal withid lóolonal wa.
   The man worked slowly.

45

(c) Bíi eril sháad be bethedi halewan wáa.
She went home in order to work.
Bíi eril sháad be bethedi héeyawáan wáa.
She went home because of fear.

Rules and Explanation:

(1) To mark a Case Phrase as an Identifier (that which identifies the subject by profession, sexual gender, nationality, etc.), add the zero ending—that is, add no ending. This is identical to the rule for Subject Case Phrases.

(2) To mark a Case Phrase as Manner (the way in which something is done), add the ending "-*nal*". This ending is much like English "-ly" as in "patiently" and "thoroughly".

(3) There are two endings used to mark a Case Phrase as the Cause of what is in the statement. One is "-*wan*", which means "in order to, for the purpose of "; the other is "-*wáan*", which means "due to, because of ".

(4) As you can see from the examples in (c) above, you can turn a verb of Láadan into a noun phrase by giving it a case-marker ending. English does the same thing, forming "abandonment" from "to abandon", "carelessness" from "to be careless", and so on; any English verb can be used as a noun if "–ing" is added, as in "Swimming is good exercise".

BRIEF READING:

Bíide eril melothel with nedelotheth[1] menedebe wáa. Eril medam[2] ben wotheth.[3] Medi ben edanádi, "Bre aril mehel nen daneth leneda, ébre aril loláad len thenath. Izh aril memíi[4] len woho." Eril medi edaná benedi, "Bíi mehan len neneth wa. Nen with, len with. Bre medúuhel len daneth witheda, ébre aril meloláad len shamath."[5]

[1] nedeloth	= fact	
[2] dam	= to show, to manifest	
[3] woth	= wisdom	
[4] míi	= to be amazed	
[5] shama	= grief for good reasons, but grief for which nobody is to blame and about which nothing can be done	

Free Translation:

Women knew many things. They showed wisdom. They said to the linguists, "If you make a language for us, we will be joyful. But we will be amazed, every one of us." The linguists said to them, "We know you. You are women, we are women. If we fail to make a language for women, we will be sorrowful—but that will just be the way things are."

Notes on the Translation:

There are of course many ways to translate the end of the reading. For example, "We hope we can do it, and we will be sorry if we can't, but all we can do is try. And if we fail that's how it goes sometimes." It's not that you cannot express in English what is expressed in Láadan by "*shama*", but it is extremely cumbersome to do so.

SUPPLEMENTAL SECTION:

(1) Bíi eril di with

shóodenal wáa.	BUSY, shóod
rahowana	COLD, rahowa
lirinal	COLORFUL, liri
menanal	MENA, compassion for good reasons
balanal	ANGER, for good reasons
ohenanal	RESPECT, for good reasons
bishibenal	SUDDEN, bishib

The woman spoke _____ ly.

(2) Bíi le

ewithá wa.	ANTHROPOLOGIST
ehashá	ASTRONOMER
emidá	BIOLOGIST
eloshá	ECONOMIST
eduthá	ENGINEER
hená	SIBLING
belidá	CARPENTER
lilahá	LOVER, one who carries out the female sexual act; not of males
yodá	DINER, one who eats
yodálh	GLUTTON, one who eats too much

I am a(n)_____ .

NOTE: You can form many useful words with the suffix "-*á*" and the

47

prefix "*e-*" shown above. ("*E-*" means "science of", something like English "–ology".) For example, you can begin with "*shon*", the word meaning "peace"; "*shoná*" means "peacemaker", "*eshon*" means "peace science", and "*eshoná*" would then be "peace scientist". Similarly, from "*om*", "to teach", we have "*omá*", teacher and "*ehom*", education and "*ehomá*"; the last refers to a specialist in education who is not herself necessarily a teacher.

(3) Bíi ril sháad be   áanawan wáa.   SLEEP, áana
                        imewan   TRAVEL, im
                        róowan   HARVEST, róo
                        rúuwan   LIE DOWN, rúu

     She's going now in order to _____.

(4) Bíi eril delishe be   olobewáan wáa.   BLOW, TRAUMA, olob
                        ibewáan   CRIME, ib
                        doshewáan   BURDEN, dosh
                        ludewáan   DEBT, lud
                        ozhewáan   DREAM, ozh
                        lodewáan   HOUSEHOLD, lod
                        uhudewáan   NUISANCE, uhud
                        éeyawáan   SICKNESS, ILLNESS

     She wept because of the _____.

48

Lesson 11

PATTERN:

[(Aux) Verb (Neg) CP-S CP-POSSESSIVE]

Vocabulary:

-tha	(POSSESSIVE ending, by birth)
-the	(POSSESSIVE ending, for no known or acknowledged reason)
-thi	(POSSESSIVE ending, by chance)
-tho	(POSSESSIVE ending, other; by law or custom or gift, etc.)
-thu	(POSSESSIVE ending; this is the "false" possessive, and is explained below)

NOTE: Because the explanation of the Possessive takes so much space, no other vocabulary is added in this section.

Examples:

(a) Báa eril ma lan netho?
    Did your friend listen?
Báa arl yod eba netho?
    Will your spouse eat?
Báa mehóoha oyi netha?
    Are your eyes tired?
Báa thal ana nethe?
    Is your food all right?

(In these sentences, your friend and your spouse are asserted to be "yours" by law or custom or something of the kind; your eyes are yours because you were born with them; and the speaker who mentions "your" food is stating that she either does not know or will not acknowledge why it should belong to you.)

(b) Bíi eril meláad len beth nethoth wa.
We saw your home.
Bíi eril mesháad len beth nethodi wa.
We went to your house.

Rules and Explanation:

(1) To use the Láadan possessive, you must first decide what sort of "ownership" is involved. Is it because of birth, as with "my arm" or "my mother"? If so, add the ending "-*tha*". Is it for no known reason—for example, a task that you just ended up with somehow, inexplicably, and that is now "your" work? Then the proper ending is "-*the*". Is it a phony ownership, marked in English by "of" but really involving no possession, as in "a heart of stone" or "a collection of books"? If so, use the ending "-*thu*". Is it by luck, by chance? Use the ending "-*thi*". In any other situation, when ownership is due to law or custom or anything not included in the other forms, use the ending "-*tho*". You would use "-*tho*" if you were not certain of the reason but were quite sure there was one and that it was legitimate.

(2) Next, realize that the Possessive will always be part of some bigger Case Phrase. When you say "He stole the jewels of the Queen", the Object is the whole sequence "the jewels of the Queen", of which "of the Queen" is only a part. This means that except for those case categories which have a zero ending in Láadan (Subject and Identifier) you will first add the possessive ending and then the case-marker ending of the larger CP. When "your house" is the Goal, and English would show that by the sequence "to your house", Láadan uses "*belid*" plus the ending "-*tho*" plus the Goal ending "-*di*", to give you "*belidethodi*". The Possessive marker will always come before the other ending.

(3) Finally, you cannot add the Possessive markers directly to the name of a person or animal. Instead, you add a pronoun to carry the case ending—like this:

(a) Bíi eril eb le belid withethoth wa.
I bought the woman's house.
(b) Bíi eril eb le belid Meri bethoth wa.
I bought Mary's house.

The sequence "*Meri bethoth*" is literally "Mary she-of-OBJECT", you see. You cannot say "*Merithoth*" to mean "Mary-of-OBJECT". (Note that this rule does not apply to names of places and of times—only living or once-living beings.)

BRIEF READING:

Bíide eril el edaná daneth wa. Eril thi dan zhath[1], Láadan. Bíi ril le nedi, "Ril nawéedan ne Láadan, dan withetho nede". Eril el edaná Láadan, izh ril ra dan edanátho wa. Bre menéde with Láadan, ébre Láadan dan witheda i withetho.

[1] zha = name

Free Translation:

Once a linguist made a language. The language had the name, Láadan. I say to you, "You are reading Láadan now, one woman's language". A linguist made Láadan, but it is not the linguist's language now. If women want Láadan, then Láadan is a language for women and of women.

Notes on the Translation:

There might be disagreement about the choice of the possessive ending in "*dan withetho nede*". Like any human language, Láadan has possible ambiguities, and this is one of them. You cannot tell from these few sentences if "*dan withetho nede*" means "one language of a woman" or "one 'woman's language'"; nor can you tell why "*-tho*" has been chosen. You know only that the speaker or writer is claiming that the ownership is not because of birth, that it is not unknown or unacknowledged, and that it is claimed to be real ownership rather than the "house of wood" sort. It may be like the situation in English when we speak of "Emily Dickinson's poems" or "the novels of Jane Austen"; there is a sense in which such things "belong" to those who make them, but it is a restricted sense. To make this reading quite clear on the subject, it would have to be longer. (The word "*Láadan*", by the way, is formed from "*láad*", to perceive; and "*dan*", language.)

51

SUPPLEMENTAL SECTION:

(1) Bóo dama ra ne

oda lethath.	ARM
oba lethath.	BODY
ona lethath.	FACE
óoda lethath.	LEG
óoyo lethath.	MOUTH
oyo lethath.	NOSE
thom lethoth.	PILLOW

Please don't touch my _____.

(2) Bíi eril

lámála	beye rul nethoth wa.	CARESS, STROKE
wem		LOSE
bel		TAKE
she		COMFORT
doth		FOLLOW
bóodan		RESCUE
naya		TAKE CARE OF

Somebody   (VERBed)   your cat.

NOTE: "*Beye*" means "somebody"—just one somebody. Like all the other pronouns, it can take the ending "-*zh*" to mean two to five persons, and the ending "-*n*" to mean many persons. It can also mean "something" and is made clear by the verb used with it.

52

Lesson 12

PATTERN: This is a lesson about embedding one sentence inside another sentence. In the examples, the embedded sentence will be enclosed in brackets to help make the process clear.

Vocabulary:

lali	(rain, or to rain)
rahowa	(to be cold)
na-	(to begin to VERB)
no-	(to cease to VERB)
lith	(to think)
bróo	(because)
-hé	(statement embedding marker)
-hée	(question embedding marker)

Examples:

(a) Bíi lith le [rahowa lalihé] wa.
      I think that the rain is cold.

(b) Bíi lith ra le [rahowa lalihé] wa.
      I don't think that the rain is cold.

(c) Báa lith ne [rahowa lalihée] ?
      Do you think that the rain is cold?

(d) Bíi lothel ra le [rahowa lalihée] wa.
      I don't know whether the rain is cold.

53

(e) Bíi lith le [nalalihé] wa.
       I think that it's starting to rain.
   Bíi lith le [nolalihé] wa.
       I think that it has stopped raining.

NOTE: Láadan does not require any "it" in the sentence to do the raining, although one will appear in the English translation.

Rules and Explanation:
   (1) To embed a declarative sentence, add the ending "-*hé*" to the last word in the sentence.
   (2) To embed a question, add the ending "-*hée*" to the last word in the sentence.
   (3) It's true that the embedded sentences in the examples above are all Objects of the verb "to think". However, it is impossible for a sentence to be doing the thinking, and there can be no misunderstanding; no "-*th*" ending is required here. If you should ever have a sentence that could be misunderstood in this way, the embedding marker will follow the case-marker ending—this is the ONLY piece that can be added to a case-marker ending, and it will very rarely be necessary.

BRIEF READING:

Bíide eríli nasháad lanemid[1] wetheha óobe wo. Eril láad be anath oyinan doniha; di be, "Wu[2] wothal wohana! Néde le beth!" I bel be anath i nawida be beth. Eril nosháad lanemid iliha. Eril láad be lanemideth i anath oyinan iliha yil.[3] Di be, "Bíi néde le beth wa!" Id eril wem[4] be anath, bróo u[5] óoyo betha. I bróo eril lanemid yodalh[6] wi.

[1] lanemid	= dog
[2] Wu	= what a.../such a...
[3] yil	= under
[4] wem	= to lose
[5] u	= to be open
[6] yodalh	= glutton

Free Translation:

Once long ago a dog was going along a road. It saw some food on the ground; it said, "What good food! I want it!" And it took the food and began to carry it. The dog stopped at some water. It saw a dog and some food under the water. It said, "I want it!" And then it lost the food, because its mouth was open. And—as anyone can see—because it was a glutton.

SUPPLEMENTAL SECTION:

(1) Bíi lothel le   owa roshehé   wa.   the sun is warm

                 oth shenidalehé   a network is important

                 lalewida withehé   the woman is (joyfully) pregnant

                 elesháana withehé   the woman is menstruating for the first time

                 zháadin withehé   the woman is menopausing

                 eril lhedahé   there was discord-in-the-home (lhed = discord-in-the-home)

                 aril rashahé   there will be discord

I know that __(SENTENCE)__ .

NOTE: Remember that in the embedded sentences above the verb will be first in the sentence, or the auxiliary will if one is present. (This is the reverse of what appears in the English translations.) The word for "network" is "*shenidal*"; the others should be clear.

Lesson 13

PATTERN: This is another lesson about embedding one sentence in another; this time we will be looking at what are called "relative clauses" in English. They will be in brackets in the examples.

Vocabulary:

elahela	(celebration)
oth	(to be important
Hathameshǎal	(Sunday)
shóo	(to happen, come to pass, take place)
dom	(to remember)
-hǎa	(relative clause embedding marker)

Examples:

(a) Bíi aril shóo elahela Hathameshǎaleya wáa.
> The celebration happens on Sunday.

Bíi oth [aril shóo elahela Hathemashǎaleyahǎa] wáa.
> The celebration that happens on Sunday is important.

(b) Bíi dom le [hal withehé] wa.
> I remember that the woman works.

Bíi dom le [hal withehǎa] wa.
> I remember the woman that works.

Rules and Explanation:

(1) To embed a sentence as a relative clause, add the ending "-*hǎa*" to the last word of the embedded sentence. (NOTE: When this ending follows the case-marking ending of PLACE, "-*ha*", it has an alternate form "-*shǎa*".)

(2) The primary purpose of the examples in (a) is to show you what is just about the longest and most complicated-appearing word (to an English speaker) that you are likely to have to deal with in Láadan. The complexity of the form is more in its appearáance than in reality, however; let's analyze "*Hathamesháaleyaháa*" to see what it's made of. You will see the root "*sháal*" in the middle of the long word and recognize it as the word for "day". "*Hathamesháal*" is equivalent to "Sunday". The TIME ending, "*-ya*", has been added, along with an "*e*" to separate the two consonants, and then the embedding marker "*-háa*" has been added to that.

(3) The purpose of the two examples in (b) is to show you why just one embedding marker won't be sufficient.

(4) It would be absurd to pretend that the grammar explanation in this lesson and Lesson 12 has been complete enough. Many more examples and explanations would be required before that claim could be made. But you will have a general overview of the embedding processes of Láadan, and would be able to understand complex sentences like these in reading and listening even if you could not comfortably construct them yourself. Their proper place in any more detailed discussion is in a more advanced grammar of the language—please do not be concerned if you are not at ease with them.

SUPPLEMENTAL SECTION:

(1) Bíi néde le   rahíya beyeháa wa.   BIG, LARGE
               éthe   CLEAN
               shane   DOWNY, FURRY
               dash   SOFT, PLIANT

I want something that is _____.

58

Lesson 14

This is the final lesson in this simple grammar; like Lessons 12 and 13, it is intended only to present material briefly so that you will be able to deal with it in reading or listening. The subject of the lesson is WH–questions (a very English term that owes its form to the fact that most English question words start with WH), questions that cannot be answered with "yes" or "no". They are very simply formed in Láadan, but look so different from their English counterparts that they are likely to be awkward for English speakers at first. I will just provide an example of each kind, which means that the format of this lesson will be unlike any of the others.

These questions begin with "*báa*" like any other question, although in speech that word may not appear when it is not necessary for clarity. (Obviously, if you want to use any of the endings that show that you ask your question in anger, or in jest, etc., you cannot drop the "*Báa*" to which those endings are attached.) Then the item of information that is being requested appears as the pronoun "*be*" or one of its plural forms, plus "*-báa*" to mark it as interrogative, followed by the proper case-marking ending. Here are the examples, for your information.

(1) Báa eril   yod bebáa   thilith?   **Who ate the fish?**
    Q   PAST EAT   SOMEBODY   FISH

NOTE: Since the Subject case ending is Ø, "*bebáa*" has no other marker. The same thing will be true for an Identifier.

(2) Báa eril yod thili bebáath?   **What did the fish eat?**
(3) Báa eril sháad ne bebáadi?   **Where did you go (to)?**
(4) Báa eril sháad ne bebáade?   **Where did you come from?**
(5) Báa eril thod ne bebáanan?   **What did you write with?**

(6) Báa eril hal ne bebáaden? Who did you work with?
(7) Báa eril hal ne bebáaya? When did you work?
(8) Báa eril hal ne bebáaha? Where did you work (at)?
(9) Báa eril hal ne bebáanal? How (in what manner) did you work?
(10) Báa eril hal ne bebáawan? Why did you work?
    Báa eril hal ne bebáawáan? Why did you work?
(11) Báa eril hal ne bebáada? Who did you work for?
(12) Báa eril wéedan ne áabe bebáathoth? Whose book did you read?
(13) Báa bebáa omá? Who is a/the teacher?

60

English to Láadan Dictionary

A

a/the-final-one	nonede
to be **able**	thad
above	rayil
absence-of-pain	shol
to be **accursed**, unholy	rahéeda
across	mesh
after	ihée
afternoon	udathihée
against	ib
agriculture	eróo
air	shum
airplane	zhazh
airport	hozhazh
ale	wéebe
to be **alien**	née
an **alien**	née; an alien (noun)=néehá
to be **alive**	wíi

to be **alone**	sholan
all, every	woho
all-power	hohathad (like "omnipotence", but without the feature MALE)
all things, all-that-is	abesh
although	íizha
always	hadiha
to be **amazed**	míi
ambulance	duthamazh
Amen	Othe
analysis	yan
anarchy	ralod
and	i
and-then	id
anesthesia	duthawish
angel	noline; angel-science=enoline
anger[1]	bara; bala; bama; bana; bina
animal, domestic	shamid
animal, wild	romid
anorexia	rayide
ape	omamid
APOLOGY	hoda=pardon me; hóoda=excuse me
apple	doyu
apricot	thuyu
April	Athil
argument, quarrel	rashon (not used of an "argument" in a theory or an equation or proposition)
Arkansas	Arahanesha (a loanword) Aranesha, "pet" name, short form
arm (the body part)	oda
around	o
to **arrive**	nósháad
to **ask**	mime
asteroid	thamehaledal
at last, finally	doól
to **attend**, be present at	ham
attend, pay attention to	hil
aunt	berídan; great-aunt=hoberídan

[1]Many nouns of emotion have a number of forms in Láadan; see Pages 132–133 for an explanation.

autumn	wemon
AUXILIARIES	(See Page 129)
as, like	zhe
to be **ashamed**	loláad lhohoth (that is, "perceive shame")

B

baby	áwith (to indicate a male infant, use the masculine suffix "id": áwithid)
baby-nurse	háwithá
back (body part)	wan
to be bad	rathal
to be **bad + good**[2]	yéshile
bag, sack, purse	dimod
baking dish	yam
balm	ub; irritant substance=rahub
bandage	duthahod
bank (financial)	loshebelid
bankruptcy	ralosh
barn	róomath
barren-one	rawóobaná
beach	sheshihoth
to bear, give birth	wóoban; birth-giver=wóobaná
to be **beautiful**	áya; of a place=hóya; of a time=háya
because	bróo
bed	dalehanawan
bee	zhomid
beetle	yum
before	ihe
beer	webe; brewer=webehá
to be **beholden**	dinime
to **believe**, believe in	edeláad

---

[2]Láadan has a number of predicates that combine polar opposites in this way, for example, to describe someone who is both bad and good at the same time.

bell	limlim[3]
benison	ath
berry	daletham
to betray	ulhad [4]
to be **big**, large	rahíya
to be **big** + **little**[5]	nóowid
bird	babí
birth (the noun)	woban
birthday	thade
to be **bitter** (taste)	rúsho
to be **black**	loyo
to be **black** + **white**	lóothi
blanket	owahúuzh
to be **blessed**, holy	othel
blow (trauma, noun)	olob
to be **blue**	leyi
boat	esh
body	oba; anatomy=ehoba; body language=dáan i oyi (idiom)

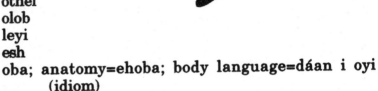

bone	thud
book	áabe
bowels	hodáath
bowl	bin
to **braid**	boóbin
brain	uth
bramble	nab
branch	odayáaninetha
bread	bal; baker=balá
to **break**	then
breast	thol
bridge	oódóo[6]
broom	wush
to be **brown**	leyan
brush	idon
brush (not for hair)	enid

---

[3]An exception to the sound rules.
[4]The word is **u** + **lh**+ **a** + **d**... the first syllable is **u**, the second **lhad**.
[5]See Note 3, above.
[6]This is a visual/aural analog form.

building	math
burden	dosh
bureaucracy	rashenhemen
to be **busy**	shóod
but	izh
butter	hob
butterfly	áalaá
to **buy**, to **sell**[7]	eb

calculator	shinishin
camel	hibomid
camera, video recorder	ridadem
callousness	raména
candy	thuhal
cape, cloak	rimáayo
car	mazh
to **caress**, stroke	lámála
carpenter	belidá
carrot	medalayun
to **carry**	wida
CASE MARKERS	(See Pages 129–130)
cat	rul
to **cause**	nin; one responsible=niná; one to blame=ninálh
cause, reason	obed
to **cause** to VERB	dó-
celebration	elahela
celibacy	rashim; a celibate=rashimá; to be celibate, by choice=lath; celibate, not by choice=ralath
center	hatham
ceremony, ritual	shun

_____

[7]For the affixes that disambiguate this form, see the Case Markers listed on Pages 129–130.

chair	dalewodewan
change	sheb; resistance to change=rasheb
cheese	ódon
chest (body part)	rawan
child	háawith
chronemics	ehath
church	áatham
circle	tham
to be clean	éthe
to be clear	wedeth
clergy	wíitham
cloak, cape	rimáayo
cloth	od; weaver=odá textile science=ehod; textile scientist=ehodá
clothing (general term)	bud
cloud	boshum
coat	habo
coffee	yob
to be cold	rahowa
to be colored, have color	liri
comb	don
to come to pass, happen	shóo
to come, go[8]	sháad
to comfort	she; comforter=sehá
command room, for war	ráatham
common sense	bash
compassion	mína, ména, móna, múna, méhéna[9]
competition	halid
computer	shinehal
comset	óozh
connection	shasho
computer printer	raneran
container	dim
contentment	nina, nena, nona, nuna, nehena[10]
cooking-pot	mahin
cooking-utensil	thibeb

_____

[8]See Case Markers on Pages 129–130 to disambiguate this form.
[9]See Note 2, Page 63.
[10]See Note 3, Page 64.

copier (like Xerox)	rimel
copulation	shim (abstract term); Note: "shimá" means "copulater", not "lover"
cordial (beverage)	yurana
to be correct	dóon
cousin	edin
coverings (bedding)	miméne
cow	dithemid
cradle	lulin
cream	onelal
creature	mid
credit, money	losh; economics=elosh; economist=eloshá; banker =loshá
crime	ib
criminal	ibalh
crowd	méwith
to cry (of babies)	wée
cup	ni
cupboard, dresser	dimidim
curtain	demeren

D

to dance	amedara
danger	rayom
darkness	rahith
day	sháal
DAYS OF THE WEEK	(See Page 135)
to be dead	rawíi
death	shebasheb
debt	lud; with negative conotation=lhud
to be deep	ruhob
desire (sexual)	maha; absence of desire=ramaha
desk	dalebediwan
despair	rathena

desert	shée
dessert	homanáa
digit (toe, finger)	ishid
to be **dirty**	rahéthe
discord	rasha (not of discord in the home)
discord-in-the-home	lhed
disgust	ílhi; also "ílhilh"[11]
dish	bod; ceramics=ebod
to **do**	shub
to **do well**, thrive	thaá
doctor, physician	eduthahá
dog	lanemid
door	áath
to **dominate**	dórado; with evil intent=dólhórado
down	heb
to be **downy**, furry	shane
dowry	heth
dream	ozh
dress, gown	owe; man's garment=owehid
to **drink**	rilin
drink, beverage	rana; drinker=ranahá; alcoholic=ranahálh
to **drop**, spill, let fall	héda
drought	ralali
drug	desh
dulcimer	shelalen
DURATION MARKERS	(See Page 130)
during	obée

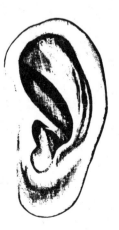

ear	oyu; audiology=ehoyu
to be **early**	dide
earth, soil, ground	doni

_____

[11]"lh" is always a negative and a pejorative.

Earth	Thera (loanword)
earthquake	donithen
earthworm	shéeba
east	hene
to eat	yod
eating-utensil	min
education	ehom
egg	máa
elephant	domid
EMBEDDING MARKERS	
	(See Page 130)
emotion	wihi[12]
emotionlessness	rawihi; not a complimentary term
empathy (total)	wohosheni
END-OF-PRAYER	Othe (used like "Amen")
enemy	leb; also "lheb"
enigma, puzzle	zhab
every	woho
evidence	meloth
EVIDENCE MORPHEMES	
	(See Page 131)
evil (theological sense)	ramíila
to exhaust oneself	ibo; ibolh
to exile	rahabelhid; an exile, outcast; rahabelhidá
to exist	in
eye	oyi

F

face (body part)	ona
fact	nedeloth
family	onida
famine	rahana
to be far	thed

[12]For Láadan, the sentence pattern for emotions is "X perceives-internally Emotion Y".

farm	ábed; farmer=ábedá
to be **fast**	ralóolo
to **fast**	dod
to **fear**	héeya
feather	hosh
to **female-sexual act**	lila; lover, female=lilahá—not used to refer to males
few, to be few	nedebe
to **fill**, fill up	lob; to become full=nolob
to **find**	redeb
final, last one	nonede
fire	óowa
fish	thili
fleecy-clouded (said of skies)	bol
floor	rabobosh
flower	mahina
flute	déethel
FOCUS MARKER	-hóo
to **follow**	doth
food	ana; nutrition=ehana; junk food=rahana
foot (body part)	óoma
"fool's gold"	rahobeyal
for-sure (emphatic)	hulehul
forever	hathehath
foremother	wohothul
forest	olin
to **forgive**	baneban
fork	batha
formalism (scientific notation)	eéden
fowl, poultry	lub
fox	dumidal
to be **fragrant**	aba
friend	lan
friendliness	dina, dena, dona, duna, dehena [13]
frost	nith
fruit	yu
to be **full**, abundant	ume

---

[13]See Note 1, Page 62.

G

gadget	rahed
game	shida
garden	déela
gas (oxygen, etc.)	wish
gate	urahu
to gather	buth (not said of people)
to gather, assemble	lolin (of people)
geometry	etham; geometrician=ethamá
to be gentle	lema
geography	ehoth
gestalt	wésha
to get, obtain	thel
to get by	thaáhel
gift	bini; gift with strings attached=rabinilh
to give	ban
glass (for drinking)	hed
globe, sphere, planet	thamehal
gloves, mittens, socks, stocking	sishida
goat	éezh
to go, come	sháad[14]
goddess, deity	Lushede
gold	obeyal
to be good	thal; of time=hathal; of place=hothal
gospel	thaledan
government	yon; administration=eyon
grain	ede
grand-daughter	hóowith; great=shinehóowith
grandmother	hothul; great=shinehothul
granary	edemath
grape	éelen
grass	hesh
gratitude	wánea, wéná, wóná, wúná, wéhená [15]

[14]See Case Markers listed on Pages 129–130 to disambiguate this form.
[15]See Note 1, Page 62.

to be **gray, grey**	líithin
to be **green**	liyen
GREETING	Wil sha (literally, "Let there be harmony")
grief	shara, shala, shama, shana, shina[16]
group	olowod
guardian	lúul
guest	thóo; hospitality=ethóo
guitar	lalen

H

hail	(weather term) hishud
hair	delith
ham radio	hidel
hand	oma
handicap	won
harbor	réele
to be **hard**, firm	radazh
harmony	sha
harvest	róo; harvester, gatherer=róohá
hat	yen
to **have**	thi; owner, possessor=thihá
head	on
to **heal**	dutha; medicine=edutha
health	lam
heart	óoya
to be **heavy**	sho
to **help**	den
herb	thesh
here	nu
to be **high**, tall	íthi
hill	hibo
hip	rum
history	eri

[16]See Note 1 Page 62.

to **hoard**	raheb
holiday	diídin
Holy-One, Deity	Lahila
holyday	shehéeda
home	beth
honey	thu; beekeeper=thuhá
hope	omid
hospital	duthahoth
hotel	both
house	belid
household	lod
housewife/ **househusband**	elodá
to **hunger**	yida
hurricane	yulehul
to **hurt**, feel pain	úuya
hypothesis	lithewil

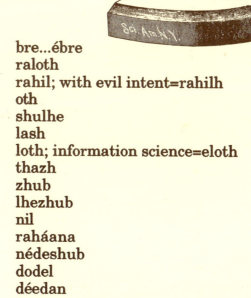

if...then	bre...ébre
ignorance	raloth
to **ignore**	rahil; with evil intent=rahilh
to be **important**	oth
inappropriate	shulhe
indifference	lash
information	loth; information science=eloth
to **inherit**	thazh
insect	zhub
noxious **insect**	lhezhub
inside	nil
insomnia	raháana
intent	nédeshub
interface	dodel
to **interpret**	déedan

intersection	sheni
investigation	ezhabá
to be irresponsible	ráhesh
irritant substance	rahub
island	mari

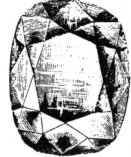

Jesus of Nazareth	Zheshu (loan word)
jewel	theda
jonquil, daffodil	léeli
joy	thina, thena, thona, thuna, thehena[17]
juice, sap	éeb
to **jump**	oób

kettle	dizh
kidney	yeb
king	unáhid; also, háhid
knife	hum
to **know** (of people)	an (as in "I know Amy")
to **know** (not people)	lothel

[17]See Note 3, Page 63.

L

lamp, light	ithedal
to **land** (as a ship or plane)	adoni (also "a landing")
language	dan
to be **last** (adjective, "final")	rush
later	aril
to **laugh**	ada
layer	bre
to **lead**	un; leader=uná
leaf	mi
to **learn**	bedi; student, learner=bedihá
LEAVETAKING, FAREWELL	Aril
leg	óoda
lemon	hezh
LET THERE BE, WOULD THAT...	Wil
lettuce	ilimeda
library	wéehoth
to **lie** down	rúu
life	wí
light	ith
to **lightning**	lish
lightning bolt	ezhahith
to be **like** (X like Y)	zhe; identical-sibling=zhehá
like, as	zhe
lilac	lehina
lime	hizh
line (of a computer program, or a line drawn on a surface)	bod
linguistics	edan; linguist=edaná
to **listen**, to listen to	ma[18]

---

[18]This verb takes Speech Act affixes optionally. See Page 132.

to **live**, inhabit	habelid
liver	web
livestock	womil
long-ago	eríli
long-ahead, far future	aríli
to **lose**	wem
love; also, to **love**	a (of inanimates only)
to **love** [19]	am, azh, áazh, ad, ab, ashon, sham, éeme, áayáa, aye
love for evil	ralhoham
lover	lilahá (not used of males)
lovingkindness	donidan; donidaná (channel for loving kindness)
lustfully, desiringly	mahanal (not a negative term)

M

machine	zhob
magic, enchantment	yahanesh
Magic Granny	Shósho (a character in stories)
to **make**	el
Mama	Emath
to **manifest**	dam (That is, to show signs of some state or emotion. Used like English "seem".)
manners, courtesy	shal
to be **many**, many	menedebe
map	luben
mattress	hóo
mead	thuwebe
meadow	dun
meal (lunch, etc.)	anadal; cook=anadalá
meat	deheni
melody	wethalehale (literally, "music path)
melon	ozhi
memory	elothel

---

[19]Láadan has numerous words for "love" of various kinds; for translations, see Pages 136.

to **menopause**	zháadin; ...uneventfully=azháadin; ...when it's welcome=elazháadin
to **menstruate**	osháana; ...for the first time=elasháana; ...early=desháana; ...late=wesáana; ...painfully=husháan; ...joyfully=sháana
mercy	yidan
meta-	lée-
milk (noun)	lal; mother's milk=lalal
mind	óoyahonetha
mineral	ba
mirror	betheb
to **mistranslate**	rahéedan; deliberately and with evil intent =rahéelhedan
mode	nub
modem	modem (loanword)
money, credit	losh
month	hathóol
MONTHS OF YEAR	(See Page 135)
moon	óol
mop	iliwush
mother	shathul (formal term=honored mother)
mother	mathul (informal intimate term)
mother's milk	lalal
mountain	bo
to **mourn**	óom
to **move**	mina; transportation=emina
mule	wothemid
to be **murky**, obscure	rawedeth
muscle	thun
mushroom	mud
to **"music"**	alehale (that is, to sing or whistle or usea musical instrument)
mystery	lush
myth	dedidewoth (literally, "story-wisdom"; does not mean untruth)

N

nail, claw (body part)	bath
name	zha
nation	shishidebeth
neck	(body part) womedim
nectar	hom
nectar food, dessert	homana
nectarine	homeyu
need -for (X)	them
to needlework	dathim
negative, no	ra
neighbor	obeth
network	shenidal
nerve	bid
neurology	ebid
never	rahadidad
nevertheless	éde
niece	sherídan; great=hosherídan
night	náal
no, not	ra (this form is also the word "No")
nobody	rawith
no how, in no way	ranal
none, not at all	rawoho
to nontouch	radama; with evil intent=radamalh
node	rad
noise	zholh
noon	udath
north	hun
to not-fit, to be wrong for	shulhe
nothing	radal
nowhere	rahoth
nuisance	uhud
NUMBERS, NUMERALS	(See Page 136)
nurse	onin
nut-tree	mal

O

to **obfuscate**	ralhewedeth
object	dale
ocean	mela; ocean-dweller=melahá
office, workplace	hohal
often	hath menedebe
oil (household)	bom
to be **old**	balin
one	nede
onion	bremeda
only	neda
to be **open**	u
or, either/or	e...e
orange (the fruit)	yun
to be **orange**	layun
ornament	dimilin
orphan	nuthul
outside, out	ranil
oven	óob
to **overflow** (as of water)	shulin
owl	húumid
owner	thihá

P

pain	heyi
paper	mel
paradise	olim
parent	thul
park	heshehoth

part (of machine, etc)	wud
pasta	ededal
peace	shon; peace-science=eshon; peace-maker=shoná; aggressor=rashonelhá
pearl	nem
penis	bom
to **perceive**[20]	láad
to **perceive-internally**[21]	lolaád
perceiver	láada
perception	láa
person	with; anthropology=ewith; anthropologist=ewithá; science of male persons=ewithid
piano	zhuth
to **pick** up, lift up	héedá
picture	dadem
pig	muda
pillow	thom
pitcher	raliha
place	hoth
to be **placid**, still	wam
plain, flat plain	rabo
planet	thamehal
plant	dala
plate	rin
PLEASE...	Lu...
to **please**	shi
poem	dáanelom
poet	dáanelom
poetics	edáanashon
poetry	edáanelom
poison	lhu
to be **poor**	shud
potato	udemeda
poultry, fowl	lub

---

[20]Láadan uses these two verbs for the concepts expressed by English "to see, to hear, to taste, etc." and for both senses of "to feel". To say in Láadan, "I see X", requires "I perceive X with my eyes"; to say "I feel the wind" requires "I perceive the wind with my flesh"; to say "I feel anger" requires "I perceive-internally anger". A literal translation of English "I am angry", for example, is not possible. Pages 129–133, Rules of Láadan Grammar, should clarify this somewhat.

[21]See Note 20, above.

power (extraordinary, omnipotence)	hohathad
praise	dithal
prayer	ohamedi
predicate	(noun)shoth
to be pregnant	lawida;
	...joyfully=lalewida;
	...wearily=lóda;
	...for the first time=lewidan;
	...late in term and eager for the end=widazhad

presence	ram
to be present	ham
price	nath
prisoner	zhilhad
program (of computer)	bodibod
PRONOUNS	(See Page 136)
proposition, argument	halith
psalm	sháam (a loan word)
to be pure, perfect	shad
to be purple	lula

quilt (not patchwork)	balish
patchwork quilt	báalish

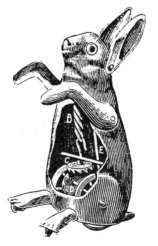

rabbit	shanemid
radiance	míili

radio	del
rain; also, to rain	lali
to **read**	wéedan
reason, cause	obed
to **record**, keep records	ri
to be **red**	laya
refrigerator	nithedim
to **regret**	zhala (grief paradigm)
to **rejoice**	lo
religion	ehéeda
to **relinquish** a cherished perception	zhaláad
to **remember**	dom

REPETITION MORPHEMES
    (See Page 131)

to **rescue**, save	bóodan
respect[22]	ohina, ohena, ohona, ohuna, ohehena
to be **responsible**	áhesh
to give **rest**, to refresh, to rest	dul
rice	ilihede
to be **rigorous**	shel
to **rise**, stand up	thib
river, creek	wili
to **rock** (of babies)	luth
rocking chair	lolin
room	shod
root	dol
rose	shahina
rug, carpet	ren
ruler, boss	hu

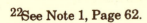

[22]See Note 1, Page 62.

to be **sacred**	héeda
to be **safe**	yom
sage, wise person	wothá
saint	lawith
salt	máan
sand	sheshi
to **say**, tell, speak	di; rhetoric=edi; speaker=dihá
school	ulin
scientist	ehá
scientifically	enal
seaweed	lel
seed	thon
seldom	hath nedebe
to **sell, buy**[23]	eb
to **send**	nori
sentence	déeladáan
to be **several**	nedebe
to **"sexual act"**	shim; one who performs a sexual act=shimá ....cannot mean "lover"
shadow	rum
shame	lhoho
to **share**	edethi
sheep	éesh
sheet (bedding)	úuzh
shelf	dob
shirt	bon
shoe	óomi
shoulder	rim
sibling-by-birth	hena
sibling-of-the-heart	héena
sickness	éeya
to **sign** (as in ASL)	lishid; signer= lishidá[24]

[23]See Case Markers, Pages 129–130, to disambiguate this form.
[24]This verb takes Speech Act affixes, optionally. See Pages 131–132 for an explanation.

silence	rile
silver	yeth
sin	lha
sink	bid
to sit	wod
skirt	áayo
sky	thosh
slave	rahulh
sleep	áana
skin, flesh	oya
to sleep	ina
to be slow	lóolo
to be small	hiya
snake	ezha
snow	hish
soap	éthedale
socks, stockings	ishida
song	lom
soul	óotha
sound	zho; aloud=zhonal
soup	thulana
to be sour	yem
south	han
space (outer)	delin
spaceliner	yoda
spaceship	yo

SPEECH ACT MORPHEMES

	(See Pages 131–132)
spice	laheb
spider	dathimemid
spine (body part)	doluth
spoon	bada
spouse	eba
spring (season of year)	wemen
stable	midemath
star	ash; astronomy=ehash

STATE-OF-CONSCIOUSNESS
MORPHEMES

STATE-OF-CONSCIOUSNESS MORPHEMES	(See Page 132)
to stay	benem

to be **still**, placid, calm (as of water, wind)	wam
to **stink**, reek	rabalh
stomach	hod
stone	ud
to **store**	ol; to waste or squander=rahol
store, market	wehe
storm	rohoro
story	dedide
stove	dimóowa
to be **strong**	do
to **study**	ulanin
SUCH A...WHAT A...	Wu...
sudden	bishib
summer	wuman
sun	rosh
to be **sweet** (taste)	meéhan (meénan)
symbol (of a notation, or an alphabet or orthography)	uzh
synergy	ru; synergist=eruhá

T

table	daleyodewan
tactile deprivation	rálámálha
to **take**	bel
to **take-away-from**	raban
to **take care of**	naya; care-giver=nayahá
tape recorder	rizho
tea	zhu
to **teach**	om; teacher=omá
telephone	widadith
television	théle (loanword)
temptation	erabalh

85

terror	eéle
testicle	hibid
THANK-YOU	áala
there	núu
therefore	owáano
thing	dal
to think	lith; psychology=elith
to thirst	yada
this/that/these/those	hi
thorn	bash
throat	wom
through	obe
thunder	lorol
thus	hinal
tick (the insect)	uhudemid
time	hath
together	shidi
toilet, W.C.	al
tool	ed
tooth	dash; dentist=edashá
to torment	rashe; to torture=rashelh
tornado	thamehal
to touch	dama[25]; science-of-touch=edama
towel	dib
town, city	miwith; city-dweller=miwithá
toy	dínídin
train	memazh
to translate	héedan
to travel	im
tray	dodi
tree	yáanin
trunk (for storage)	yomedim
truth, honor	shadon
to try to X	du- plus verb; try to speak=dudi
to try in vain to X	dúu- plus verb; try in vain to speak=dúudi
trousers, pants	inad
tulip	hodo
turtle, tortoise	balinemid

[25]This form takes Speech Act affixes. See Pages 131–132 an explanation.

to be **two**　　　　shin
typewriter　　　ran

U

to be **ugly**　　　　modi
under　　　　　　yil
underground　　　than
to **understand**　　en; philosophy=ehen
underwear　　　　hem
unfriendliness　　radena
to be **united**　　　shishid
up　　　　　　　raheb
to **use**　　　　　　duth

V

vacuum cleaner　　éthedal
vagina　　　　　　lul
valley　　　　　　yed
vegetable　　　　meda
vehicle　　　　　razh
vine　　　　　　thil
violet　　　　　oyimahina
violin　　　　　dóolon
voice　　　　　dith

W

to **want**	néde
war	rashonelh
wardrobe	budim
warehouse, storehouse	dalemath
to be **warm**	owa
washcloth	éthehod
wasp	resh
to **waste**, squander	rahol
to **watch**, pay attention	il
water	ili
wave	aáláan
way, road, path, etc.	weth
to be **weak**	rado
to **wear**	une
to be **weary**	óoha
weather	ro
weed	nish
week	híyahath
to **weep**	delishe (not said of infants)
WELL...	Dóo...
west	hon
to be **wet**	lili
whale	uthemid
to be **white**	líithi
widow	sheba
will (theological)	yoth
wind	yul
window	dem; someone you can see right through=demá
wine	rushi
winter	weman
wire	widáahith
wisdom	woth; sage, wise one=wothá
without	raden
wood	bosh
word	dáan

work, also to work	hal
work counter, surface	behal
WOULD THAT, LET THERE BE...	Wil...
to write	thod
wrinkle (in skin)	zháa
writing-implement	dalethodiwan; short form=thodi

(no entries at this time)

to be yellow	léli
yes	em
to be yielding, pliant	dazh
to be young	rabalin
YOU'RE WELCOME	Oho

(no entries at this time)

Láadan to English
Dictionary

(Based on work done by Karen Robinson; used with permission)

As is true in the translation from any language into another, many words of Láadan cannot be translated into English except by lengthy explanation.

We wish to note that the pejorative element "*lh*" can always be added to a word to give it a negative connotation, so long as it precedes or follows a vowel and does not violate the rules of the Láadan sound system by creating a forbidden cluster. The addition of "*lh*" need not create an actual new word; for example, "*awith*" means "baby"—to use instead "*lhawith*" (or "*awithelh*") means only something like "the darned baby" and is ordinarily a temporary addition. But it is very handy indeed; we are indebted to the Navajo language for this device.

a	love (for inanimates only; to love (inanimates only)
áa be	book
áa la	THANK-YOU
áa laá	butterfly

91

aáláan	wave
áana	sleep [ina=to sleep]
áath	door
áatham	church [áath=door + tham=circle]
áayáa	mysterious love, not yet known to be welcome or not
áayo	skirt
áazh	love for one sexually desired at one time, but not now
ab	love for one liked but not respected
aba	fragrant
ábed	farm
ábedá	farmer [áabed=farm + -á=agent, doer]
abesh	all things, all-that-is
ad	love for one respected but not liked
ada	to laugh
Adaletham	August (berry month) [daletham=berry]
Adol	December (root month) [dol=root]
adoni	to land (as a ship or plane); also a landing [doni=earth]
Ahede	September (grain month) [ede=grain]
áhesh	to be responsible
Ahesh	March (grass month) [hesh=grass]
al	toilet
alehale	to make music
Alel	January (seaweed month) [lel=seaweed]
am	love for one related by blood
Amahina	May (flower month) [mahina=flower]
Ameda	July (vegetable month) [meda=vegetable]
amedara	to dance
an	to know (of people)
ana	food
anadal	meal (lunch, dinner, etc) [ana=food + dal=thing]
anadalá	cook [anadal=meal + -á=suffix for doer]
aril	FUTURE, (time aux) [aril=later]
aril	later
Aril	LEAVETAKING, FAREWELL [aril=later]
aríli	FAR FUTURE (time aux)
ash	star
ásháana	to menstruate joyfully [oshaána=to menstruate]

ashon	love for one not related by blood, but heart-kin
ath	benison
Athesh	June (herb month) [thesh=herb]
Athil	April (vine month) [thil=vine]
Athon	November (seed month) [thon=seed]
áwith	baby, infant [with=person]
áwithid	male baby, male infant [áwith=baby + -id=suffix for male]
áya	to be beautiful
ayáanin	February (tree month) [yáanin=tree]
aye	love that is unwelcome and a burden
Ayu	October (fruit month) [yu=fruit]
azh	love for one sexually desired now
azháadin	to menopause uneventfully [zháadin=to menopause]

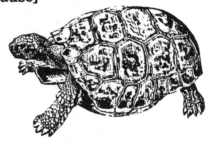

báa	QUESTION
báalish	patchwork quilt [balish=quilt, not patchwork]
babí	bird
bad	mineral
bada	spoon
bal	bread
balá	baker [bal=bread + -á=suffix for doer]
bala	anger with reason, with someone to blame, which is futile [bala, bana, bama, bina=anger]
balin	old
balinemid	turtle, tortoise [literally, old creature]
balish	quilt, not patchwork
bama	anger with reason, but with no one to blame, which is not futile [bala, bana, bara, bina=anger]
ban	to give
baba	anger with reason, with no one to blame, which is futile [bara, bala, bama, bina=anger]

babeban	to forgive
bara	anger with reason, with someone to blame, which is not futile [bala, bama, bana, bina=anger]
bash	common sense
bash	thorn
bath	nail, claw (body part)
bath	six
batha	fork
bathethab	sixteen [bath=6 + thab=10]
bé	PROMISE [speech act morpheme]
bedi	to learn
bedihá	student, learner [bedi=learning + á=suffix for doer]
bée	WARNING [speech act morpheme]
behal	work counter, surface [hal=work]
bel	to take
belid	house
belidá	carpenter [belid=house + -á=suffix for doer]
benem	to stay
berídan	aunt
beth	home
betheb	mirror
bid	sink
bid	nerve
bíi	DECLARATIVE [speech act morpheme]
bim	four (4)
bimethab	fourteen (14) [bim=4 + thab=10]
bin	bowl
bina	anger with no reason, with no one to blame, which is not futile [bara, bala, bama, bana=anger]
bini	gift
bishib	sudden
bo	mountain
bó	COMMAND [speech act morpheme] (very rare except to small children)
bod	line (on a surface or of a computer program)
bod	dish
bodibod	program (computer) [bod=line + i=and]
bol	fleecy-clouded (of skies)
bom	penis
bom	oil (household)

bon	shirt
bóo	REQUEST [speech act morpheme; usual "command" form]
boó	three (3)
boóbin	to braid [boó=three]
bóodan	to rescue, save
boóthab	thirteen (13) [boó=3 + thab=10]
bosh	wood
boshum	cloud (bo=mountain + shum=air)
both	hotel
bre	layer
bre...ébre	if...then
bremeda	onion [bre=layer + meda=vegetable]
bróo	because
bud	clothing (general term)
bud	nine (9)
budethab	nineteen (19) [bud=9 + thab=10]
budim	wardrobe [bud=clothing + dim=container]
buth	to gather (not used with people)

D

dáan	word [dan=language]
dáanashoná	poet
dáanelom	poem
dadem	picture
dal	thing
dala	plant
dale	object
dalebediwan	desk [dale=object + bedi=learning + -wan=suffix for purpose, in order to]
dalehanawan	bed [dale=object + ana=sleep + -wan=suffix for purpose, in order to]
dalemath	warehouse, storehouse [dale=object + math =building]

daletham	berry [dala=plant + tham=circle]
dalethodiwan	writing implement [dale=object + thodi=to write + −wan=suffix for purpose, in order to]
dalewodewan	chair [dale=object + wod=to sit + -wan=suffix for purpose, in order to]
daleyodewan	table [dale=object + yod=to eat + -wan=suffix for purpose, in order to]
dam	to manifest, to show signs of some state or emotion
dama	to touch
dan	language [dáan=word]
dash	tooth
dathim	to needlework
dathimemid	spider
dazh	to be yielding, pliant, soft
debe	one-hundred (100)
debe i nede	one-hundred-and-one (101) [debe=100 + i=and + nede=1]
dedide	story
dedidewoth	myth [dedide=story; woth=wisdom]
déedan	to interpret [dan=language]
déela	garden
déeladáan	sentence
déethel	flute
dehena	friendliness, despite negative circumstances [dena, dina, dona, duna=friendliness]
deheni	meat
del	radio
delin	space (outer)
delishe	to weep (not said of babies)
delith	hair
dem	window
demá	someone you can see right through [dem=window + −á=suffix for doer]
demeren	curtain [dem=window; ren=rug, carpet]
den	to help
dena	friendliness for good reason [dehena, dina, dona, duna=friendliness]
desh	drug
desháana	to menstruate early [osháana=to menstruate]
di	to say, tell, speak

dib	towel
dide	to be early
dihá	speaker [di=to say; -á=suffix for doer]
diídin	holiday
dim	container
dimidim	cupboard, dresser [dim=container]
dimilin	ornament
dimod	bag, sack, purse [dim=container]
dimóowa	stove [dim=container + óowa=fire]
dina	friendliness for no reason [dehena, dena, dona, duna=friendliness]
dínídin	toy
dineme	to be beholden
dith	voice
dithemid	cow [literally, voice creature]
dizh	kettle
do	to be strong
dob	shelf
dod	to fast
dodel	interface
dodi	tray
dol	root
óolhorado	to dominate with evil intent [dórado=to dominate + lh=negative connotation]
doluth	spine (body part)
dom	to remember
domid	elephant [literally, remember creature]
don	comb
dona	friendliness for foolish reasons [dehena, dena, dina, duna=friendliness]
doni	earth, soil, ground
donidaná	lovingkindnesser, one who channels lovingkindness [donidan=lovingkindness +-á=suffix for doer]
donithen	earthquake [doni=earth + then=to break]
dóo	WELL.... [PHRASE]
doól	at last, finally
doóledosh	pain or loss which comes as a relief by virtue of ending the anticipation of its coming [doól=at last + dosh=burden]

dóolon	violin
dóon	to be correct
dórado	to dominate
doroledim	This word has no English equivalent whatsoever. Say you have an average woman. She has no control over her life. She has little or nothing in the way of a resource for being good to herself, even when it is necessary. She has family and animals and friends and associates that depend on her for sustenance of all kinds. She rarely has adequate sleep or rest; she has no time for herself, no space of her own, little or no money to buy things for herself, no opportunity to consider her own emotional needs. She is at the beck and call of others, because she has these responsibilities and obligations and does not choose to (or cannot) abandon them. For such a woman, the one and only thing she is likely to have a little control over for indulging her own self is FOOD. When such a woman overeats, the verb for that is "doroledim". (And then she feels guilty, because there are women whose children are starving and who do not have even THAT option for self-indulgence...)
dosh	burden
doth	to follow
doyu	apple [do=strong + yu=fruit]
du-[plus verb]	try to VERB
dul	to give rest, to refresh
dumidu	fox [mid=creature]
dun	meadóow, field
duna	friendliness for bad reasons (see "friendliness")
duth	to use
dutha	to heal
duthahá	healer [dutha=to heal + -á=suffix for doer]
duthahod	bandage [dutha=to heal + od=cloth]
duthahoth	hospital [dutha=to heal + hoth=place]
duthamazh	ambulance [dutha=to heal + mazh=car]

dúu [plus verb]	to try in vain to VERB [du- =to try to VERB]

E

e...e	or, either/or
eb	to buy, sell
eba	spouse
ebid	neurology [e-=prefix for science of + bid=nerve]
ebod	ceramics [e-=prefix for science of + bod=dish]
ed	tool
edeláad	to believe, believe in [láad=to perceive]
edama	science of touch [e-=prefix for science of + dama=touch
edan	linguistics [e=prefix for science of + dan=language]
edaná	linguist [edan=linguistics + á=suffix for doer]
edáanashon	poetics (the science of poetry)
edáanelom	poetry
edash	dentistry [e-=prefix for science of + dash=tooth]
ede	grain
éde	nevertheless
ededal	pasta [ede=grain + dal=thing]
edemath	grainery [ede=grain + math=building]
edethi	to share [thi=to have]
edi	rhetoric [e-=prefix for science of + di=speak]
edin	cousin
eduth	engineering [e=prefix for science of + duth=to use]
eduthá	engineer [eduth=engineering + -á=suffix for doer]
edutha	medicine [e-=prefix for science of + dutha=to heal]
eduthahá	doctor, physician, healer [edutha=medicine + —á=suffix for doer]
éeb	juice, sap
eéden	formalism, scientific notation
eéle	terror
éelen	grape
éeme	love for one neither liked nor respected

99

éesh	sheep
éeya	sickness
éezh	goat
ehá	scientist [e-=prefix for science of + -á=suffix for doer]
ehana	nutrition [e-=prefix for science of + ana=food]
ehash	astronomy [e-=prefix for science of + ash=star]
ehath	chronography [e-=prefix for science of + hath=time]
ehéeda	religion [e-=prefix for science of + héedáa=sacred]
ehen	philosophy [e-=prefix for science of + en=to understand]
ehoba	anatomy [e-=prefix for science of + oba=body]
ehod	textile science [e-=prefix for science of + od=cloth]
ehom	education [e-=prefix for science of + om=to teach]
ehoth	geography [e-=prefix for science of + hoth=place]
ehoyu	audiology [e-=prefix for science of + oyu=ear]
el	to make
elahela	celebration [alehale=to make music]
elasháana	to menstruate for the first time [oshana=to menstruate]
elazháadin	to menopause when it's welcome [zháadin=to menopause]
elith	psychology [e-=prefix for science of + lith=think]
elodá	housewife/househusband [e-=prefix for science of + lod=household + á=suffix for doer]
elosh	economics [e-=prefix for science of + losh=money, credit]
eloth	information science [e-=prefix for science of + loth=information]
elothel	memory [eloth=information science]
em	yes [INTERJECTION]
Emath	Mama [mathul=mother] (intimate, informal)
emid	biology [e-=prefix for science of + mid=creature]
emina	transportation [e-=prefix for science of + mina=to move]
en	to understand
enid	brush (not for hair)
enoline	angel-science [e-=prefix for science of + noline=angel]
erabalh	temptation

100

eri	history [e-=prefix for science of + ri=to keep records]
eril	PAST (time aux.) [eri=history]
eríi	FAR PAST, LONG AGO (time aux.) [eri=history]
eróo	agriculture [e-=prefix for science of + róo=harvest]
eruhá	synergist [e-=prefix for science of + ru=synergy + á=suffix for doer]
esh	boat
eshon	peace-science [e-=prefix for science of + shon=peace]
etham	geometry [e-=prefix for science of + tham=circle]
éthe	to be clean
éthedal	vacuum cleaner [éhe=clean + dal=thing]
éthehod	washcloth [éthe=clean + od=cloth]
ethoo	hospitality [e-=prefix for science of + thoo=guest]
ewith	anthropology [e-=prefix for science of + with=person]
ewithid	science of males [e-=prefix for science of + with=person + -id=suffix for male]
eyon	administration [e-=prefix for science of + yon=government]
ezha	snake
ezhahith	lightning bolt [ezha=snake + ith=light]

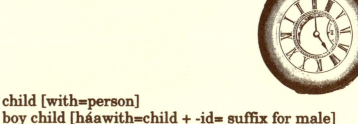

H

háawith	child [with=person]
háawithid	boy child [háawith=child + -id= suffix for male]
habelid	to live, inhabit [(belid=house]
habo	coat
hadidad	always
hahod	to be in a state of
halá	worker [hal=work + -á=suffix for doer]
halith	proposition, argument
ham	to attend, to be present at
han	south

Haneshául	Thursday (South Day) [han=south + sháal=day]
hath	time
hath menedebe	often [hath=time + menedebe=many]
nath nedebe	seldom [hath=time + nedebe=few]
hathal	to be good [said of time]
hatham	center [tham=circle]
Hathameshául	Sunday (Center Day) [hatham=center + sháal=day]
hathehath	forever, time everlasting [hath=time]
hathóol	month [hath=time + óol=moon]
háwithá	baby nurse [áwith=baby + -á=suffix for doer]
háya	to be beautiful (said of time) [áya=to be beautiful]
heb	down
hed	glass (for drinking)
héda	to drop, spill, let fall [héeda=to pick up, lift up]
héedá	to pick up, lift up [héda=to drop, let fall]
héeda	to be sacred
héedan	to translate [dan=language]
héeya	to fear
hem	underwear
hemen	bush
hena	sibling by birth [héena=sibling of the heart]
hene	east
Heneshául	Monday (East Day) [hene=east + sháal=day]
hesh	grass
heshehoth	park [hesh=grass + hoth=place]
heth	dowry
heyi	pain
hezh	lemon [hizh=lime]
hi	this, that, these, those
hibid	testicle
hibo	hill [híya=small + bo=mountain]
hibomid	camel [hibo=hill; mid=creature]
hidel	ham radio [híya=small + del=radio]
hinal	thus [hi=this, that + -nal=suffix for manner]
hish	snow
hishud	hail [hish=snow + ud=stone]
híya	to be small
híyahath	week [híya=small + hath=time]
hizh	lime [hezh=lemon]
hob	butter

hoberídan	great-aunt [berídan=aunt]
hod	stomach
hoda	APOLOGY (pardon me) [phrase]
hodáath	bowels [hod=stomach + áath=door]
hodo	tulip
hohal	office, workplace [hal=to work]
hohathad	all-power, omnipotence [thad=to be able]
hom	nectar
homana	nectar food [hom=nectar + ana=food]
homeyu	nectarine [hom=nectar + yu=fruit]
hon	west
Honesháal	Tuesday (West Day); [hon=west + sháal=day]
hóo	mattress
hóoda	APOLOGY (excuse me) [phrase] [hoda=APOLOGY]
hoówith	granddaughter [with=person]
hoówithid	grandson [with=person + -id=suffix for male]
hosh	feather
hosherídan	great niece [sherídan=niece]
hoth	place
hothal	to be good [said of place]
hothul	grandmother [thul=parent]
hóya	to be beautiful (said of place) [áya=to be beautiful]
hozhazh	airport [zhazh=airplane]
hu	ruler, boss
hulehul	for sure (an emphatic, strong positive) [phrase] [–hul=suffix denoting to an extreme degree]
hum	knife
hun	north
Hunesháal	Wednesday (North Day) [hun=north + sháal=day]
husháana	to menstruate painfully [osháana=to menstruate]
húumid	owl húu (onomatopoeia) [mid=creature]

I

i   and

ib	crime; against
ibálh	criminal [ib=crime + -á=suffix for doer + lh =negative connotation]
ibo	to exhaust oneself
id	and-then
idon	brush (for hair)
ihe	before [ihée=after]
ihée	after [ihe=before]
íizha	although
il	to watch, pay attention
ílhi	disgust [lh=negative connotation]
ílhilh	disgust with pejorative overtones, disgust and disapproval [lh=negative connotation]
ili	water
ilihede	rice [ili=water + ede=grain]
ilimeda	lettuce [ili=water + meda=vegetable]
iliwush	mop [ili=water + wush=broom]
im	to travel
in	to exist
ina	to sleep [áana=sleep]
inad	trousers, pants
ishid	digit (fingers, toes)
ishida	gloves, mittens, socks [ishid=digit (finger, toe]
ith	light
ithedal	lamp, light [ith=light + dal=thing]
íthi	to be high, tall
izh	but

L

láa	perception [láad=to perceive]
láad	to perceive [láa=perception]
laheb	spice
Lahila	Holy-One, Deity
lal	milk

104

lalal	mother's milk
lalen	guitar
lalewida	to be pregnant joyfully [lawida=to be pregnant]
lali	rain, to rain [lil=water]
lam	health
lámála	to caress, stroke
lan	friend
lanemid	dog [lan=friend + mid=creature]
lash	indifference
lath	to be celibate by choice
lawida	to be pregnant
lawith	saint [Lahila=Holy-One + with=person]
laya	to be red
layun	to be orange
leb	enemy
lée-	meta- [prefix]
lehina	lilac (the flower, bush)
lel	seaweed
léli	to be yellow
lem	to be gentle
lewidan	to be pregnant for the first time [lawida=to be pregnant]
leyan	to be brown
leyi	to be blue
lha	sin [lh=negative connotation]
lheb	enemy, with pejorative overtones [leb=enemy + lh=negative overtones]
lhed	discord in the home [lh=negative connotation]
lhezhub	noxious insect [lh=negative connotation + zhub=insect]
lhoho	shame [lh=negative connotation]
lhu	poison [lh=negative connotation]
lhud	debt, with pejorative overtones [lh=negative connotation + lud=debt]
líithi	to be white
líithin	to be gray
lila	to female-sexual-act
lilahá	lover (female only) [lila=to female sexual act + −á=suffix for doer]
lili	to be wet [lil=water]

limlim	bell [onomatopoeia]
liri	to be colored
lish	to lightning
lishid	to sign (as in ASL)
lishidá	signer (as in ASL) [lishid=to sign + -á=suffix for doer]
lith	to think
lithewil	hypothesis [lith=to think + Wil...=LET THERE BE]
liyen	to be green
lo	to rejoice
lob	to fill, fill up
lod	household
lóda	to be pregnant wearily [lawida=to be pregnant]
loláad	to perceive internally, to feel [láad=to perceive]
loláad lhohoth	to be ashamed, to perceive one's shame [lolaad=to perceive internally + lhoho=shame + -th =suffix for object]
lolin	to gather, assemble (said of people)
lolin	rocking chair
lom	song
lóolo	to be slow
lóothi	to be black and white
lorolo	thunder
losh	credit, money
loshá	banker [losh=money + -á=suffix for doer]
loshebelid	bank (financial) [losh=money + belid=house]
loth	information
lothel	to know (not of people) [loth=information]
lowitheláad	to feel, as if directly, another's pain/joy/ anger/grief/surprise/ etc.; to be empathetic, without the separation implied in empathy [with=person + láad=to perceive]
loyo	to be black
Lu...	PLEASE...[phrase]
lub	poultry, fowl
luben	map
lud	debt
lul	vagina
lula	to be purple
lulin	cradle [lul=vagina]

lush	mystery
Lushede	deity, goddess (informal address)
luth	to rock (of babies)
lúul	guardian

M

ma	to listen, to listen to
máa	egg
máan	salt
máanan	to be salty
maha	desire (sexual)
mahanal	desiringly, lustfully (NOT a negative term) [maha=desire (sexual) + -nal=suffix for manner]
mahin	cooking pot
mahina	flower
mal	nut-tree
mari	island
math	building
mathul	mothul (intimate informal term, but not Mama) [ma=to listen + thul=parent]
mazh	car, automobile
meda	vegetable
medalayun	carrot [meda=vegetable + layun=orange]
méehan	to be sweet
méhéna	compassion despite negative circumstances [ména, mína, móna, múna=compassion]
mel	paper
mela	ocean [(ili=water + me-=implies greater weight or size or importance]
melahá	ocean-dweller [mela=ocean + -á=suffix for doer]
meloth	evidence [loth=information + me-=implies greater weight or size or importance]

memazh	train [mazh=car + me-=implies greater weight or size or importance]
ména	compassion for good reasons [méhéna, mína, móna, múna=compassion]
menedebe	to be many [nedebe=to be few + me-=implies grater weight or size or importance]
merod	billion (1,000,000,000) [rod=million (1,000,000) + me-=implies greater weight or size or importance]
mesh	across
méwith	crowd [with=person + me-=implies greater weight or size or importance]
mi	leaf
mid	creature
midemath	stable [mid=creature + math=building]
míi	to be amazed
míili	radiance [míi=to be amazed]
mime	to ask
miméne	coverings, bedding
min	eating utensil
mina	to move
mína	compassion for no reason [ména, méhéna, móna, múna=compassion]
miwith	town, city [with=person]
miwithá	city-dweller [miwith=city + -á=suffix for doer]
modem	modem [loanword]
modi	to be ugly
móna	compassion for foolish reasons [méhéna, ména, mína, múna=compassion]
mud	mushroom
muda	pig
múna	compassion for bad reasons [méhéna, ména, mína, múna=compassion]

náal	night
nab	bramble
nath	price
naya	to take care of
nayahá	care-giver [naya=to take care of + -á=suffix for doer]
neda	only [nede=one]
nede	one, (1)
néde	to want
nedebe	to be few
nedebe	to be several [but not many]
nedeloth	fact [nede=1 + loth=information]
nédeshub	intent
nedethab	eleven (11) [nede=1 + thab=10]
née	to be alien
néehá	alien [née=to be alien + -á=suffix for doer]
nehena	contentment despite negative circumstances [nena, nina, nona, numa=contentment]
nem	pearl
nena	contentment for good reasons [nehena, nina, nona, nuna=contentment]
ni	cup
nib	eight (8)
nibethab	eighteen (18) [nib=8 + thab=10]
nil	inside
nin	to cause, causal
nina	contentment for no reason [nehena, nena, nona, nuna=contentment]
niná	the one responsible [nin=to cause + -á=suffix for doer]
ninálh	the one to blame [niná=the one responsible + lh=negative connotation]
nish	weed
nith	frost
nithedim	refrigerator [nith=frost + dim=container]

noline	angel
nolob	to become full [no-=prefix implies completion + lob=to fill up, to fill]
nona	contentment for foolish reasons [nehena, nena, nina, numa=contentment]
nonede	a/ the final one [no-=prefix implies completion + nede=one, 1]
nóowid	to be big and little
nori	to send
nósháad	to arrive [no-=prefix implies conpletion + sháad=to come, go]
nótháa	to cease to thrive [no-=prefix implies completion + tháa=to thrive, to do well]
nu	here
nub	mode
núháam	to feel oneself cherish, cared for, nurtured by someone
nuna	contentment for bad reasons [nehena, nena, nina, nona=contentment]
nuthul	orphan [thul=parent]
núu	there [nu=here]

o	around
oba	body
obe	through
obed	cause, reason
obée	during
obeth	neighbor
obeyal	gold
od	cloth
odá	weaver
oda	arm (the body part)

odayáaninetha	branch [oda=arm + yáanin=tree + -tha=suffix for possession by reason of birth]
ódon	cheese
oham	love for that which is holy
ohamedi	prayer [oham=love for that which is holy + di=to say, speak]
ohehena	respect despite negative circumstances [ohena, ohina, ohona, ohuna=respect]
ohena	respect for good reasons [ohehena, ohina, ohona, ohuna=respect]
Oho	YOU'RE WELCOME [phrase]
ohona	respect for foolish reasons [ohena, ohena, ohina, ohuna=respect]
ohuna	respect for bad reasons [ohehena, ohena, ohina, ohona=respect]
ol	to store
olim	paradise
olin	forest
olob	blow (trauma)
olowod	group
om	to teach
omá	teacher [om=to teach + -á=suffix for doer]
oma	hand
omamid	ape [oma=hand + mid=creature]
omid	horse [mid=creature]
on	head
ona	face (the body part)
onelal	cream [on=head + lal=milk]
onida	family
onin	nurse
oób	to jump
óob	oven
óoba	leg
oódóo	bridge
óoha	to be weary
óol	moon
óom	to mourn
óoma	foot (the body part)
óomi	shoe [óoma=foot]

óotha	soul
óothanúthul	spiritual orphanhood, being utterly bereft of a spiritual community [óotha=soul + nuthul=orphan]
óowa	fire
óoya	heart
óoyahonetha	mind [óoya=heart + ho=head + -tha=suffix for possession by reason of birth]
óozh	comset
osháana	to menstruate, menstrual
oth	to be important
Othe	END-OF-PRAYER (like Amen or Selah) [phrase]
othel	to be blessed, holy
owa	to be warm
owáano	therefore
owahúuzh	blanket [owa=to be warm + úuzh=bedding, overing]
owe	dress, gown
owehid	men's garment [owe=dress + -id=suffix for male]
oya	skin, flesh
oyi	eye
oyu	ear
ozh	dream
ozhi	melon

R

ra	no, not
ra-	non- [prefix]
ra-ráahedethi	to be unable to feel lowitheláad, to be empathically impaired [ra=non- + edethi=to share]
ráahedethilh	to be unwilling to feel lowitheláad above; to be deliberately empathically impaired [ráahedethi=to be unable to feel lowitheláad + lh=negative connotation]
ráalehale	to be musically or euphonically deprived

ráatham	command room (for war)
radazh	to be hard, firm
rabalh	to stink, reek [ra=non- + aba=to be fragrant + lh=negative connotation]
rabalin	to be young [ra=non- + balin=to be old]
raban	to take away from [ra=ono- + ban=to give]
rabinilh	gift with strings attached [ra=non- + bini=gift + lh=negative connotation]
rabo	plain, flat plain [ra=non- + bo=mountain]
rabobosh	floor [ra=non- + bo=mountain + bosh=wood]
rad	node
radal	nothing [ra=non- + dal=thing]
radama	to non-touch, to actively refrain from touching [ra=non- + dama=to touch]
radamalh	to non-touch with evil intent [radama=to non-touch + lh=negative connotation]
radéela	non-garden, a place that has much flash and glitter and ornament, but no beauty [ra=non- + déela=garden]
raden	without
radena	unfriendliness for good reasons [ra=non- + dena=friendliness for good reasons]
radíidin	non-holiday, a time allegedly a holiday but actually so much a burden because of work and preparations that it is a dreaded occasion; especially when there are too many guests and none of them help
radina	unfriendliness for no reason [ra=non- + dina= friendliness for no reason]
rado	to be weak [ra=non- + do=to be strong]
radodelh	non-interface, a situation which has not one single point in common on which to base interaction, often used of personal relationships [ra=non- + dodel=interface + lh=negative connotation]
radona	unfriendliness for foolish reasons [ra=non- + dona=friendliness for foolish reasons]
raduna	unfriendliness for bad reasons [ra=non- + duna=friendliness for bad reasons]

113

raduth	to non-use, to deliberately deprive someone of any useful function in the world, as in enforced retirement or when a human being is kept as a plaything or a pet [ra=non- + duth=to use]
raháana	insomnia [ra=non- + áana=sleep]
rahabelhid	to exile [ra=non- + habelid=to live, inhabit + lh=negative connotation]
rahabelhidá	exile [rahabelhid=to exile + -á=suffix for doer]
rahadidad	never [ra=non- + hadidad=always]
rahana	junk food [ra=non- + ana=food]
rahana	famine [ra=non- + ana=food]
raheb	up [ra=non- + heb=down]
raheb	to hoard [ra=non- + eb=to buy, sell]
rahed	gadget, useless non-tool [ra=non- + ed=tool]
rahéeda	to be accursed, unholy [ra=non- + héeda=to be sacred]
rahéedan	to mistranslate [ra=non- + héedan=to translate]
rahéena	non-heart-sibling, one so entirely incompatible with another that there is no hope of ever achieving any kind of understanding or anything more than a truce, and no hope of ever making such a one understand why; (does not mean "enemy") [ra=non- + héena =sibling of the heart]
rahéelhedan	to deliberately mistranslate with evil intent [rahéedan=to mistranslate + lh=give negative connotation]
rahesh	to be irresponsible [ra=non- + ahesh=to be responsible]
rahéthe	to be dirty [ra=non- + éthe=to be clean]
rahib	non-crime, a terrible thing done because it's necessary but for which there is no blame because there is no choice (never an accident); [ra=non- + ib=crime]
rahil	to non-attend, ignore, withhold attention [ra=non- + il=pay attention to]
rahilh	to non-attend, ignore, withhold attention with evil intent rahil=to withhold attention + lh= gives negative connotation]

rahith	darkness [ra=non- + ith=light]
rahíya	to be big, large [ra=non- + híya=to be small]
rahobeth	non-neighbor, one who lives nearby but does not fulfill a neighbor's role (not necessarily pejorative)
rahobeyal	fool's gold [ra=non- + obeyal=gold]
rahol	to waste, squander [ra=non- + ol=to store]
rahom	to non-teach, to deliberately fill students' minds with empty data or false information; (can be used only of persons in a teacher/student relationship); [ra=non- + om=to teach]
rahoth	nowhere [ra=non- + hoth=place]
rahowa	to be cold [ra=non- + owa=to be warm]
rahu	to be closed [ra-non- + u=to be open]
rahub	irritant substance [ra=non- + ub=balm]
rahulh	slave [ra=non- + hu=ruler + lh=negative connotation]
raláad	to non-perceive [ra=non- + láad=to perceive]
raláadá	non-perceiver; one who fails to perceive [raláad=to non-perceive + -á=suffix for doer]
raláadálh	non-perceiver, one who fails to perceive deliberately and with evil intent [raláadá=non-perceiver + lh=negative connotation]
ralaheb	something utterly spiceless, "like warm spit", repulsively bland and blah [ra=non- + laheb=spice]
ralali	drought [ra=non- + lali=rain]
ralámálha	tactile deprivation [ra=non- + lámála=to caress + lh=negative connotation]
ralée-	non-meta [prefix], something absurdly or dangerously narrow in scope or range
ralhewedeth	to obfuscate [ra=non- + wedeth=to be clear + lh=negative connotation]
rahoham	love for evil [ra=non- + oham=love for that which is holy]
raliha	pitcher
ralith	to deliberately refrain from thinking about something, to wall it off in one's mind by deliberate act [ra=non- + lith=to think]
ralod	anarchy [ra=non- + lod=household]

ralóolo	to be fast [ra=non- + lóolo=to be slow
ralorolo	non-thunder, much talk and commotion from one (or more) with no real knowledge of what they're talking about or trying to do, something like "hot air" but more so [ra=non- + lorolo=thunder]
ralosh	bankruptcy [ra=non- + losh=money]
raloth	ignorance [ra=non- + loth=information]
ram	presence
ramaha	absence of desire [ra=non- + maha=desire (sexual)]
ramána	callousness for good reasons [ra= non- + mena=compassion for good reasons]
ramíila	evil (theological) [ra=non- + míili=radiance]
ramime	to refrain from asking, out of courtesy or kindness [ra=non- + mime=to ask]
ramimelh	to refrain from asking, with evil intent; especially when it is clear that someone badly wants the other to ask [ramine=to refrain from asking + lh=give negative connotation]
ramína	callousness for no reason [ra-non- + mína=compassion for no reason]
ramóna	callousness for foolish reasons [ra=non- + móna=compassion for foolish reasons]
ramúna	callousness for bad reasons [ra=non- + múna=compassion for bad reasons]
ran	typewriter
rana	drink, beverage
ranahá	drinker [rana=drink + -á=suffix for doer]
ranahálh	alcoholic [ranahá=drinker + lh=negative connotation]
ranal	no how, in no way [ra=non- + -nal=suffix for manner]
ranem	non-pearl, an ugly thing one builds layer by layer as an oyster does a pearl, such as a festering hatred to which one pays attention [ra=non- + nem=pearl]
raneran	computer printout [ran=typewriter]
rani	non-cup, a hollow accomplishment, something one acquires or receives or accomplishes but is empty of all satisfaction [ra=non- + ni=cup]

116

ranil	outside, out [ra=non- + nil=inside]
rarilh	to deliberately refrain from recording; for example, the failure throughout history to record the accomplishments of women [ra=non- + ri=to record, keep records + lh=negative connotation)
rarulh	non-synergy, that which when combined only makes things worse, less efficient, etc. [ra=non- + ru=synergy + lh=negative connotation]
rasha	discord (not discord in the home) [ra=non- + sha=harmony]
rashe	to torment [ra=non- + she=comfort]
rasheb	resistence to change [ra=non- + sheb=change]
rashelh	to torture [rashe=to torment + lh=negative connotation]
rashenidal	bureaucracy [ra=non- + shenidal=network]
rashida	non-game, a cruel "playing" that is a game only for the dominant "player" with the power to force others to participate [ra=non- + shida=game]
rashim	celibacy [ra=non- + shim=to sexual act]
rashimá	a celibate [rashim=celibacy + -á=suffix for doer]
rashon	argument, quarrel [ra-non- + shon=peace]
rashonelh	war [rashon=quarrel + lh=negative connotation]
rashonelhá	aggressor [rashonelh=war + -á=suffix for doer]
rathal	to be bad [ra=non- + thal=to be good]
rathena	despair for good reasons [ra=non- + thena=joy for good reasons]
rathina	despair for no reason [ra=non- + thina=joy for no reason]
rathom	non-pillow, one who lures another to trust and rely on them but has no intention of following through, a "lean on me so I can step aside and let you fall" person [ra=non- + thom=pillow]
rathona	despair for foolish reasons [ra=non- + thona=joy for foolish reasons]

rathóo	non-guest, someone who comes to visit knowing perfectly well that they are intruding and causing difficulty [ra=non- + thóo=guest]
rathuna	despair for bad reasons [ra=non- + thuna=joy for bad reasons]
rawan	chest (body part)
rawedeth	to be murky, obscure [ra=non- + wedeth=to be clear]
raweshalh	non-gestalt, a collection of parts with no relationship other than coincidence, a perverse choice of items to call a set; especially when used as "evidence" [wesha=gestalt + lh=negative connotation]
rawihi	emotionlessness (NOT a complimentary term) [ra=non- + wihi=emotion]
rawíi	to be dead [ra=non- + wíi=to be alive]
rawith	nobody [ra=non- + with=person]
rawoho	none, not at all [ra=non- + woho=all]
rawóobaná	barren one [ra-non- + wóobaná=birth giver]
rayida	anorexia [ra=non- + yida=hunger]
rayil	above [ra=non- + yil=under]
Rayilesháal	Friday (Above Day) [rayil=above + sháal=day]
rayom	danger [ra=non- + yom=safe]
razh	vehicle
redeb	to find
réele	harbor
ren	rug, carpet
resh	wasp
ri	to record, keep records
ridadem	camera, VCR [ri=to record + dadem=picture]
ril	PRESENT [Time Auxilliary]
rile	silence
rilin	to drink
ririli	HYPOTHETICAL (would, might, let's suppose...) [Time Auxilliary]
rim	shoulder
rimáayo	cloak, cape [rim=shoulder + áayo=skirt]
rimel	copier (like Xerox) [ri=to record + mel=paper]
rim	plate

rizho	tape recorder [ri=to record + zho=sound]
ro	weather
rod	million (1,000,000)
rohoro	storm [ro=weather]
romid	wild animal [mid=creature]
róo	harvest
róohá	harvester, gatherer [róo=harvest + -á=suffix for doer]
róomath	barn [róo=harvest + math=building]
rosh	sun
ru	synergy
ruhob	to be deep
rul	cat
rum	hip
rumi	shadow
rush	to be last, final
rushi	wine
rúsho	to be bitter (to taste)
rúu	to lie down

S

sha	harmony
sháad	to come, go
sháadehul	growth through transcendence, either of a person, a non-human, or thing (for example, an organization, or a city, or a sect) [sháad=to come, go + -hul=suffix denoting to an extreme degree]
sháal	day
sháam	psalm [loanword]
shadon	truth [sha=to be perfect, pure + don=head]
shahina	rose
shal	manners, courtesy

shala	grief with reason, with blame, and futile [shama, shane, shara, shine=grief]
sham	love for the child of one's body, presupposing neither love nor respect nor their absence
sham	five (5)
shama	grief with reason, but with no blame, and not futile [shala, shana, shara, shina=grief]
shamethab	fifteen (15) [sham=5 + thab=10]
shamid	domestic animal [sha=harmony + mid=creature]
shana	grief with reason, but with no blame and futile
shane	to be downy, furry
shanemid	rabbit [shane=furry + mid=creature]
shara	grief with reason, with blame, and not futile [shala, shama, shana, shina=grief]
shasho	connection
shathul	mother (formal term, honored mother) [sha=harmony + thul=parent]
she	to comfort
sheb	change
sheba	widow [sheb=change + eba=spouse]
shebasheb	death [sheb=change]
shée	desert
shéeba	earthworm
shehá	comforter [she=to comfort + -á=suffix for doer]
shehéeda	holy day [she=to comfort + héeda=to be sacred]
shel	to be rigorous
shelalen	dulcimer
sheni	intersection
shenidal	network [sheni=intersection + dal=thing]
sherídan	niece
sheshi	sand
sheshihoth	beach [sheshi=sand + hoth=place]
shi	to please
shida	game [shi=to please]
shidi	together
shim	to "sexual act"
shimá	one who performs a sexual act (cannot mean lover) [shim=to "sexual act" + -á=suffix for doer]
shim	to be two, two (2)

shina	grief without reason or blame, not futile [shala, shama, shana, shara=grief]
shinehal	computer [shin=two + hal=to work]
shinehóowith	great granddaughter [shin=two + hóowith=grand daughter]
shinehothul	great grandmother [shin=two +hothul=grand mother]
shinethab	twelve (12) [shin=2 + thab=10]
shinishin	calculator [shin=2 + i=and + shin=2]
shineshid	to be invited
shishidebeth	nation
sho	to be heavy
shod	room
shol	absence-of-pain
sholan	to be alone
shon	peace
shoná	peacemaker [shon=peace + -á=suffix for doer]
shóo	to come to pass, to happen
shóod	to be busy
ShóShó	Magic Granny
shoth	predicate
shub	to do
shud	to be poor
shulhe	to not fit, to be wrong for [lh=negative connotation]
shulin	to overflow, as water does
shum	air
shun	ceremony, ritual

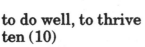

T

Tháa	to do well, to thrive
thab	ten (10)
thabebath	sixty (60)
thabebath i nede	sixty-one (61)
thabebim	forty (40)

thabebóo	thirty (30)
thabebud	ninty (90)
thabenib	eighty (80)
thabesham	fifty (50)
thabeshin	twenty (20)
thamum	seventy (70)
thad	to be able
thade	birthday
thal	be good
thaledan	gospel [thal=good; dan=language]
tham	circle
thamehal	globe, sphere, planet [tham-circle + hal=work]
thamehaledal	asteroid [thamehal=globe + dal=thing]
thameyul	tornado [tham=circle + yul=wind]
than	underground
thazh	to inherit, inherited
thed	far, to be far
thede	jewel
thehena	joy despite negative circumstances [thena, thina, thona, thuma=joy]
thel	to get, obtain
théle	television [loanword]
them	need-for X
then	to break, broken
thene	joy for good reasons [thehena, thina, thona, thuna=joy]
thera	Earth, Terra [loanword]
thesh	herb
thi	to have
thib	to rise up, stand up
thibeb	cooking utensil
thihá	owner, possessor [thi=to have]
thil	vine
thili	fish
thini	joy for no reason [thehena, thena, thona, thuna=joy]
thob	one thousand (1,000)
thob i nede	one thousand and one (1,001)
thod	to write, written
thode	writing instrument; short form of delethodiwan

thol	breast
thom	pillow
thon	seed
thona	joy for foolish reasons [thehena, thena, thina, thuna=joy]
thóo	guest
thosh	sky
thu	honey
thud	bone
thuhá	beekeeper [thu=honey]
thuhal	candy
thul	parent
thulana	soup [thul=parent + ana=food]
thun	muscle
thuna	joy for good reasons [thehena, thena, thina, thona=joy]
thuwebe	mead [thu=honey + webe=beer]
thuyu	apricot [thu=honey + yu=fruit]

U

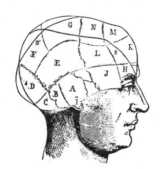

u	open
ub	balm
ud	stone
udath	noon
udathihée	afternoon [udath=noon + ihée=after]
udemeda	potato [ud=stone + meda=vegetable]
uhud	nuisance
uhudemid	tick (insect; literally, nuisance-creature)
ul	hope
ulanin	to study [ulin=school]
ulhad	to betray [lh gives negative connotation]
ulin	school
um	seven (7)
ume	to be full, abundant

umethab	seventeen (17)
un	to lead
uná	leader
une	to wear
urahu	gate [u=to be open + rahu=to be not open]
uth	brain
uthemid	whale [uth=brain + mid=creature]
úuya	to hurt, feel pain
úuzh	sheet bedding
uzh	symbol (of notation or alphabet)

wa	known to X because perceived by X [EVIDENCE MORPHEME]
wáa	assumed true by X because X trusts source [EVIDENCE MORPHEME]
waá	assumed false by X because X distrusts source [EVIDENCE MORPHEME]
waáh	assumed false by X because X distrusts source and X suspects source of acting with evil intent [EVIDENCE MORPHEME]
wam	placid, still
wan	back (body part)
we	perceived by X in a dream [EVIDENCE MORPHEME]
web	liver
webe	beer [wéebe=ale]
webeha	brewer [webe=beer]
wedeth	clear
wée	cry (of babies) [onomatopoeia]
wéebe	ale [webe=beer]
wéedan	to read [dan=language]
wéehoth	library [wéedan=to read + hoth=place]
wehe	store, market

wehena	gratitude despite negative circumstances [wena, wina, wona, wuna=gratitude]
wem	to lose
weman	winter
wemen	spring (season)
wemon	autumn
wena	gratitude for good reasons [wehena, wina, wona, wuna=gratitude]
wesha	geshalt
weshάana	to menstruate late [oshάana=to menstruate]
weth	road, way, path
wethalehale	melody (literally, music path)
wi	known to X because self-evident [EVIDENCE MORPHEME]
wí	life
wida	to carry
widάahith	wire
widadith	telephone [wida=to carry + dith=voice]
widazhad	to be pregnant late in term and eager for the end [wida=to carry + lawida=to be pregnant]
wihi	emotion
wíi	alive, living [wí=life]
wíitham	clergy [wíi=living + tham=circle]
wil	LET THERE BE..., WOULD THAT...
Wil sha	GREETING, Let there be harmony [wil=let there be + sha=harmony]
wili	river, creek [ili=water]
wina	gratitude for no reason [wehena, wena, wona, wuna=gratitude]
wish	gas (oxygen, nitrogen, etc.)
with	person
withid	male person [with=person + -id=suffix for male]
wo	imagined or invented by X, hypothetical [EVIDENCE MORPHEME]
woban	birth
wod	to sit
woho	all, every

wohosheni	a word meaning the opposite of alienation; to feel joined to, part of someone or something without reservations or barriers [woho=all; sheni=intersection]
wohothul	foremother [woho=all + thul=parent
wom	throat
womedim	neck (body part) [wom=throat + dim=container]
womil	livestock
won	handicap
wona	gratitude for foolish reasons [wehena, wena, wina, wuna=gratitude]
wonewith	to be socially dyslexic; uncomprehending of the social signals of others [won=handicap + with=person]
wóo	indicates that X states a total lack of know ledge as to the validity of the matter [EVIDENCE MORPHEME]
wóoban	to give birth, to bear
wóobaná	birth-giver [wóoban=to give birth]
woth	wisdom
wothá	sage, wise person
wothemid	mule [literally, wisdom-creature]
wu...	SUCH A..., WHAT A...
wud	part (of a machine, etc)
wuman	summer
wuna	gratitude for bad reasons [wehena, wena, wina, wona=gratitude]
wush	broom

yáanin	tree
yada	thirsty, thirsting
yahanesh	magic, enchantment
yam	baking dish

yan	analysis
yeb	kidney
yed	valley
yem	sour (to taste)
yen	hat
yéshile	to be bad and good
yesh	silver
yida	to hunger, hungry
yidan	mercy
yil	under, below
Yilesháal	Saturday [Below Day]
yo	spaceship
yob	coffee
yob	to eat
yoda	spaceliner [yo=spaceship]
yodá	diner, one who eats [yod=to eat]
yodálh	glutton [yodá=diner + lh=negative connotation]
yom	safe
yomedim	trunk (for storage) [yom=safe + dim=container]
yon	government
yoth	will (theological)
yu	fruit
yul	wind
yulehul	hurricane [yul=wind + -hul=suffix denoting to an extreme degree]
yum	beetle
yun	orange (the fruit)
yurana	cordial (the beverage) [yu=fruit + rana=drink]

Z

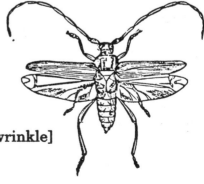

zha	name
zháa	wrinkle (in skin)
zháadin	to menopause [zháa=wrinkle]
zhab	enigma, puzzle

zhaláad	the act of relinquishing a cherished/comforting/familiar illusion or frame of perception [zha=name + láad=to perceive]
zhazh	airplane
zhe	to be like, similar
zhehá	identical sibling [zhe=like]
zhilhad	prisoner
zho	sound (audible)
zhob	machine
zholh	noise [zho=sound + lh=negative connotation]
zhomid	bee [literally, sound-creature]
zhonal	aloud [zho=sound + -nal=suffix for manner]
zhu	tea
zhub	insect
zhuth	piano

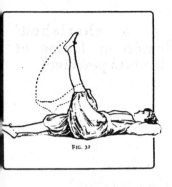

Fig. 32

Rules of Láadan Grammar

Auxiliaries:

Present	ril	Distant Past	eríli
Past	eril	Distant Future	aríli
Future	aril	Hypothetical	rilrili
Optative	wil		

Case Markers:

1. Subject   Ø
2. Identifier   Ø
3. Object   -th
4. Source   -de
5. Goal   -di, -dim
6. Beneficiary
   - -da   voluntarily
   - -dáa   obligatorily, as by duty
   - -daá   accidentally
   - -dá   by force, against X's will
7. Associate
   - -den   neutral form
   - -dan   with pleasure
8. Time   -ya
9. Place   -ha, -sha
10. Manner   -nal
11. Instrument   -nan
12. Cause
    - -wan   purpose; in order to
    - -wáan   reason; because of

13. Possessive

-tha	by reason of birth
-thi	by reason of chance
-the	for unknown or unackowledged reasons
-thu	partitive (false possessive)
-tho	other (purchase, gift, law, custom, etc.)

NOTE: Case Markers are attached to noun phrases; when no ambiguity is possible, they are optional—for example, in "I speak Láadan" no ambiguity can occur because languages cannot "speak" persons; therefore, the object marker of "Láadan" may be used or not, as the speaker wishes.

Degree Markers:

1. to a trivial degree, slightly	-hel
2. to a minor degree, rather	-hil
3. to an ordinary degree	-∅
4. to an unusual degree, very	-hal
5. to an extreme degree	-hul
6. to an extraordinary degree	-háalish

NOTE: There is an additional set of these forms restricted entirely to negative contexts, and another restricted to positive contexts. Since they would require extensive discussion, they will not be listed here.

Duration Markers:

1. to start to Verb	na-
2. to continue to Verb	ná-
3. to repeat	ne-
4. to finish, complete	no-
5. to cease to Verb	nó-

Embedding Markers:

There are three of these in Láadan. To embed a sentential complement (like English "I know that she left", where "that she left" is embedded), the suffix "–hé" is used. To embed a relative clause (like English "I know the woman who is tired"), the suffix "–háa" is used. To embed a question (like English "I wonder whether/if she left"), the suffix "–hée" is used. The embedding markers are attached to the last element in the embedded clause.

Evidence Morphemes:

1. wa   known to X because perceived by X, externally or internally
2. wi   known to X because self-evident
3. we   perceived by X in a dream
4. wáa   assumed true by X because X trusts source
5. waá   assumed false by X because X distrusts source; if evil intent is also assumed, the form is "waálh"
6. wo   imagined or invented by X, hypothetical
7. wóo   used to indicate that X states a total lack of knowledge as to the validity of the matter
8. Ø   used when X makes no comment on validity, either because of personal preference or because no comment is needed (as in a series of sentences in connected discourse)

NOTE: These morphemes are the final word in a Láadan sentence, and are used to make clear the basis upon which the utterance is offered. If none is used, and the context is not one in which the word would be redundant, the speaker is making an overt statement of refusal to supply these forms; that is allowed, but it cannot be easily overlooked. Note that these forms make direct contradiction (like English "I'm cold..." followed by "Oh, you are not," as a response) impossible.

Repetition Morphemes:

1. bada   repeatedly, at random
2. badan   repeatedly, in a pattern over which humans have no control
3. brada   repeatedly, in a pattern fixed arbitrarily by human beings
4. bradan   repeatedly, in a pattern fixed by humans by analogy to some phenomenon (such as the seasons)
5. bradá   repeatedly, in what appears to be a pattern but cannot be demonstrated or proved to be one

Speech Act Morphemes:

Declarative   Bíi (usually optional)
Question   Báa
Command   Bó (very rare, except to small children
Request   Bóo (usual "command" form)
Promise   Bé
Warning   Bée

NOTE: These forms are the first word in a Láadan sentence. There is a set of suffixes which may be attached to them to further specify the speaker/writer's intentions, as follows:

1. said neutrally   Ø
2. said in anger   -d
3. said in pain   -th
4. said in love   -li
5. said in celebration   -lan
6. said in jest   -da
7. said in fear   -ya
8. said in narrative   -de
9. said in teaching   -di

State of Consciousness Morphemes:
(The root , "be in a state of..." is "*hahod*")
1. neutral   Ø
2. ecstasy   -iyon
3. deliberately shut off to all feeling   -ib
4. in a sort of shock, numb   -ihed
5. linked empathically with others   -itha
6. in meditation   -o
7. in hypnotic trance   -óo
8. in bewilderment/astonishment, positive   -imi
9. in bewilderment/astonishment, negative   -imilh

Noun Declensions:
For those nouns which, like "grief" or "anger" or "joy", have numerous forms, there are two patterns.

<u>First Declension</u> (which always includes the affix "-*na*"):
      for no reason   -i
      for good reason(s)   -e
      for foolish reason(s)   -o
      for bad reason(s)   -u
      despite negative circumstances   -(e)he

      EXAMPLE: "joy" thina, thena, thona, thuna, thehena

Second Declension (Most easily presented as a matrix):

	-ara	-ala	-ama	-ana	-ina
REASON	+	+	+	+	−
BLAME	+	+	−	−	−
FUTILITY	+	−	+	−	−

EXAMPLE: "anger" bara, bala, bama, bana, bina

"Bina" would be an anger for which no reason can be offered, for which no blame can be attributed, but which is not futile anger because something can be done about the matter.

Word Order:

For full details, see the Grammar Lessons. However, the basic order of a Láadan sentence is as follows: Speech Act Morpheme, followed optionally by an Auxiliary, followed by a Verb, followed by one or more Noun Phrases—with Subject preceding Object—followed by an Evidence Morpheme. No distinction is made between "verbs" and "adjectives" in Láadan.

Morphology:

This section does not provide all the regularly derived forms in the language. (Again, see the Grammar Lessons.) However, we have tried to present sufficiently numerous examples of regular processes or word formation to allow the reader to predict many additional forms. For example, sets like "dan" (language) with the prefix "e-" (science of) to form "linguistics" and the agentive suffix "-á" to form "linguist" are found throughout the Dictionary section. The negative prefix "ra-" will also be obvious. We want to point out that Láadan does not permit any consonant clusters, or any sequences of more than one vowel where neither vowel has a tone marker; when combining morphemes would result in such a sequence, the language inserts "h" to break up forbidden vowel sequences, and "e" to break up forbidden consonant sequences. Thus "education" (from "om", "to learn") is not "eom" but "ehom".

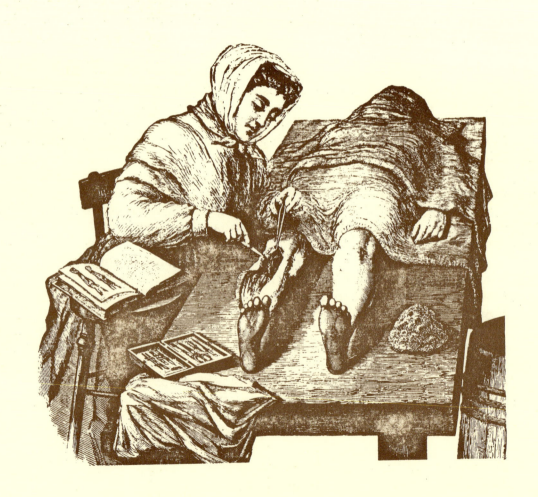

Miscellaneous Additional Information

Days of the Week, with English Equivalents:

Monday	Henesháal	East Day
Tuesday	Honesháal	West Day
Wednesday	Hunesháal	North Day
Thursday	Hanesháal	South Day
Friday	Rayilesháal	Above Day
Saturday	Yilesháal	Below Day
Sunday	Hathamesháal	Center Day

Months of the Year, with English Equivalents:

January	Alel	Seaweed Month
February	Ayáanin	Tree Month
March	Ahesh	Grass Month
April	Athil	Vine Month
May	Amahina	Flower Month
June	Athesh	Herb Month
July	Ameda	Vegetable Month
August	Adaletham	Berry Month
September	Ahede	Grain Month
October	Ayu	Fruit Month
November	Athon	Seed Month
December	Adol	Root Month

Set of "Love" Nouns:

áayáa	mysterious love, not yet known to be welcome or unwelcome
áazh	love for one sexually desired at one time, but not now
ab	love for one liked but not respected
ad	love for one respected but not liked
am	love for one related by blood
ashon	love for one not related by blood, but kin of the heart
aye	love that is unwelcome and a burden
azh	love for one sexually desired now
éeme	love for one neither liked nor respected
oham	love for that which is holy
sham	love for the child of one's body, presupposing neither liking nor respect nor their absence

Numbers, Numerals:

1. nede	11. nedethab
2. shin	12. shinethab
3. boó	16. bathethab
4. bim	20. thabeshin
5. shan	21. thabeshin i nede
6. bath	30. thabeboó
7. um	100. debe
8. nib	101. debe i nede
9. bud	1000. thob (one million is "rod")
10. thab	1001. thob i nede (one billion is "merod")

Pronouns:

	Singular	Several	Many
1. 1st person neutral	le	lezh	len
beloved	la	lazh	lan
honored	li	lizh	lin
despised	hele	lhelezh	lhelen
2. 2nd person neutral	ne	nezh	nen
(and so on as above)			
3. 3rd person neutral	be	bezh	ben
(and so on as above)			

NOTE: These are the base forms, to which the Case Markers are added. Thus "I" is "le", "me" is "leth", and so on.

	Singular	Several	Many
4. Demonstratives	hi	hizh	hin

5. Indefinites: use the base form, plus "-ye-", plus Case Marker.
6. Reflexives: use the base form, plus "-yóo-", plus Case Marker.
7. Interrogatives: use the base form, plus "-báa-", plus Case Marker.

Birthsong

(to the tune of "House of the Rising Sun")

Láadan
Thi with lometh nede neda
Bedi be lom wobameya—
Woshana wolom,
Woshana wolom,
Meshulhe dáan lometha

English
A woman has only one song,
The song she learns at birth.
A sorrowing song,
A sorrowing song—
Words don't <u>fit</u> her birthsong.

<u>Morpheme-By-Morpheme Translation</u>:

Thi	with	lometh	nede	neda
HAVE	WOMAN	SONG-OBJ	ONE	ONLY—

Bedi	be	lom	wobameya—
LEARN	SHE	SONG	BIRTH-AT (TIME)

Woshana	wolom,	woshana	wolom
[REL-GRIEF	REL-SONG	REL-GRIEF	REL-SONG]

Meshulhe	dáan	lometha.
{PL-[NOT-FIT]	WORD	SONG-OF-BY-BIRTH}

The Lord's Prayer

Láadan

Bíili,

Thul lenetha Na[1] olimeha.

Wil héeda zha Natha.

Wil nosháad sha Natha lenedi.

Wil shóo yoth Natha,

Doniha zhe olimeha;

Wil ban Na bal lenethoth lenedi

I wil baneban Na lud lenethoth lenedi

Zhe mebane len ludá lenethoth lenedi

I wil un ra Na lelneth erabal hedi

Izh wil bóodan Na leneth ramíilade

Bróo sha, sha Natha

I hohathad, hohama Natha

I hohama, hohama Natha

Ril i aril i rilrili.

Othe.

English

Our Parent,

You are in heaven.

May Your Name be holy.

May Your Harmony come upon us.

May Your will come to pass

on Earth as in heaven.

May You give us our bread.

May You forgive us our debts

as we forgive our debtors.

And lead us not ito temptation

but deliver us from evil.

For Harmony, it is Yours,

Power, it is Yours,

Glory, it is Yours,

Forevermore.

Amen.

Morpheme-By-Morpheme Translation:

Bíili

I SAY TO YOU, IN LOVE:

Thul	**lenetha**
PARENT	WE(MANY)-OF, BY BIRTH

()	**Na**	**olimeha**
BE	YOU	HEAVEN-AT

---

[1]The form "*na*" is a second person pronoun meansing "beloved you/thou"; the capital "*N*" indicates reverence for the deity.

Wil héeda zha Natha
LET-IT-BE HOLY NAME YOU-OF

Wil nosháad sha Natha lenedi
LET-IT-BE ARRIVE HARMONY YOU-OF US (MANY)-TO

Wil shóo yoth Natha,
LET-IT-BE COME-TO-PASS WILL YOU-OF

doniha zhe olimeha;
EARTH-AT AS HEAVEN-AT

Wil ban Na bal lenethoth lenedi
LET-IT-BE GIVE YOU BREAD WE (MANY)-OF-OBJ WE (MANY)-TO

i wil baneban Na lud lenethoth lenedi
AND LET-IT-BE FORGIVE YOU DEBT WE(MANY)-OF-OBJ WE (MANY)-TO

zhe mebane len ludá lenethoth lenedi
AS PL-FORGIVE WE (MANY) DEBTOR WE (MANY)-OF-OBJ WE (MANY)-TO

i wil un ra Na leneth erabalhedi
AND LET-IT-BE LEAD NEG YOU WE(MANY)-OBJ TEMPTATION-TO

izh wil bóodan Na leneth ramíilade
BUT LET-IT-BE RESCUE YOU WE (MANY)-OBJ EVIL-FROM

Bróo
BECAUSE

Sha, sha Natha
HARMONY HARMONY YOU-OF

i hohathad, hohathad Natha
AND POWER POWER YOU-OF

i hohama, hohama Natha
AND GLORY GLORY YOU-OF

ril i aril irilrili
FOREVERMORE

Othe.
AMEN.

141

Sháam 100

Láadan

Bíidi, shishidibeth woho: bóo mehel
nen wothema wozhoth Lahila Ladim.
Bóo nen donidaná Lahila Lada
themanan; Bóo mesháad nen
Hamehamedim lomedan; Bóo melothel
nen: La Lahila; La Elá len onida
Lahila Latha i len mid mededebe
naya La benethe háa. Bóo mesháad
nen urahudim Latha áaladan i
mesháad nen déeladim dithaledan
meloláad nen áalath Ladim i medi
nen othel zha Latha. Bróo thal
Lahila; hathehath yidan Latha; i
hathehath shadon Latha. (Wáa.)

English

Make a joyful noise unto the Lord,
All ye lands. Serve the Lord with
gladness; come before His presence
with singing. Know ye that the Lord
He is God: It is He that has made
us and not we ourselves; we are His
people and the sheep of His pastures.
Enter into His gates with
Thanksgiving and into His courts
with praise; be thankful unto Him
and bless His name. For the Lord is
good; His mercy is everlasting,
and His truth endureth unto all
generations.

Morpheme-By-Morpheme Translation

Bíidi,	shishidibeth	woho:
I-SAY TO YOU,	IN TEACHING, NATIONS	ALL

bóo	mehel	nen	wothema	wozhoth	Lahila	Ladim.
IMP	PL-MAKE	PL-YOU	REL-JOY	REL-SOUND	HOLY-ONE	X-GOAL

Bóo	nen	donidaná	Lahila	Lada	themanan
IMP	PL-YOU	LK-ERS[2]	HOLY-ONE	X-FOR	JOY-INSTR

Bóo	mesháad	nen	Hamehamedim	lomedan
IMP	PL-GO	PL-YOU	HOLY-PRESENCE-GOAL	SONG-ASSOC PLEASURE

---

[2]LK-ERS = Lovingkindnessers

Bóo melothel nen: La Lahila; La Elá;
IMP PL-KNOW PL-YOU: HOLY-ONE   MAKER

     len   onida Lahila Latha
     WE-PL FAMILY HOLY-ONE POSS.

     i len   mid   menedebe
     AND WE-PL CREATURE MANY

     naya   La   bebethe   háa
     TAKE CARE OF [X] THEY-MANY OBJ-REL

Bóo mesháad nen urahudim Latha áaladan
IMP GO-PL   YOU-PL GATE-GOAL POSS   THANKS-ASSOC

  i mesháad nen   déeladim dithaledan
  AND GO-PL   YOU-PL GARDEN-GOAL PRAISE-ASSOC

     meloláad nen   áalath Ladim
     PL-PERCEIVE YOU-PL THANKS-OBJ X-GOAL

     i medi nen   othel zha Latha
     AND PL-SAY YOU-PL BLESSED NAME X-POSS

Bróo thal Lahila; hathehath yiden Latha;
FOR   GOOD HOLY-ONE FOREVER   MERCY X-OF

     i hathehath shadon Latha.
     AND FOREVER   TRUTH   X-OF

         (Wáa.)
    EVIDENCE MORPHEME: TRUSTED SOURCE

Sháam 23

Láadan

Lahila nayahá letha. Aril loláad ra le
themath, rahath. Dórúu Ba leth
mewoliyen woduneha. Dódoth Ba leth
mewowam wowiliha; Dónetháa Ba
óotha lethath. Dódoth Ba leth weth
donidanethuha, zha Bathada. Iizha im
le Yed Rawithu obe, em, Aril héeya
ra le rathaleth, bróo Na leden.
Meshe dáan Natha i oyi Natha leth.
Ban Na anath i ranath ledi, íizha
meham leb letho. Boóbin Na delith
lethath oma Nathanan, shulin ni
letho. Aril mesháad thal i mena
leden, sháal woho wi lethu; i aril
habelid le lod Lahila Bathaha
ril i aril i rilrili.
OTHE.

English

The Lord is my shepherd, I shall not
want. He makes me lie down in green
pastures. He leads me beside still
waters; He restores my soul. He leads
me in paths of righteousness for His
name's sake. Even though I walk
through the valley of the shadow of
death, I fear no evil; for thou art
with me; thy rod and thy staff, they
comfort me. Thou preparest a table
before me in the presence of my
enemies. Thou annointest my head
with oil, my cup overflows. Surely
goodness and mercy shall follow me,
all the days of my life; and I shall
dwell in the house of the Lord
forever. Amen.

Morpheme-By-Morpheme Translation

Lahila	nayahá	letha
HOLY-ONE	CAREGIVER	I-OF

Aril	loláad	ra	le	themeth,	rahath.
FUTURE	PERCEIVE	NEG	I	WANT+OBJ	NEVER

Dórúu	Ba[3]	leth	mewoliyen	woduneha.
CAUSE-TO-TO-LIE-DOWN X		I-OBJ	PL-REL-GREEN	REL-FIELD-IN

Dódoth	Ba	leth	mewowam	wowiliha;
CAUSE-TO-FOLLOW X		I-OBJ	PL-REL-STILL	REL-WATER-AT

---

[3] "*Ba*" is the third-person version of "na"; a pronoun, meaning beloved He, She, or It, all at once.

144

Dónetháa   **Ba**   **óotha**   **lethath**.
CAUSE-TO-THRIVE-AGAIN   X   SOUL   I-OF-OBJ

Dódoth   **Ba**   **leth**   **weth**   **donidanethuha,**
CAUSE-TO-FOLLOW   X   I-OBJ   WAY   LOVINGKINDNESS-OF-IN

           zha Bathada.
           NAME   X-OF-FOR

Iizha   **im**   **le**   **Yed**   **Rawithu**   **obe,**   **em,**
ALTHOUGH   TRAVEL   I   VALLEY   DEATH-OF   THROUGH   YES

Aril   **héeya**   **ra**   **le**   **rathaleth,**   **bróo**   **Na**   **leden**
FUT   FEAR   NEG   I   EVIL-OBJ   FOR   THOU   I-WITH

     Meshe   **dáan**   **Natha**   **i**   **oyi**   **Natha leth.**
     PL-COMFORT   WORD   THOU-OF   AND   EYE   THOU-OF   I-OBJ

        Ban   **Na**   **anath**   **i**   **ranath**   **ledi,**
        GIVE   THOU   FOOD-OBJ   AND   DRINK-OBJ   I-TO

          íizha   **meham**   **leb letho**
          ALTHOUGH   PL-BE-PRESENT   ENEMY   I-OF

Boóbin   **Na**   **delith**   **lethath**   **oma**   **Nathanan,**
BRAID   THOU   HAIR   I-OF-OBJ   HAND   THOU-OF-WITH

        shulin   **ni**   **letho**
        OVERFLOW   CUP   I-OF

    Aril   **mesháad**   **thal**   **i**   **menaleden,**
    FUTURE   GO   GOODNESS   AND   COMPASSION-WITH

      sháal   **woho**   **wi**   **lethu;**
      EVERY   DAY   I-OF   LIFE

I   **aril**   **habelid**   **le**   **lod**   **Lahila**   **Bathaha**
AND   FUTURE   DWELL   I   HOUSEHOLD   HOLY-ONE   X-OF-IN

     ril i aril i rilrili
     FOREVER

     OTHE.
     AMEN

146

Lesson #1

Wohiya Wodedide ShóSho Bethu
(A Little Story About Magic Granny)

Bíide eril wod i alehale Shósho wo. Eril aba i owa sháal; eril tháa déela betho; loláad Shósho thena wo. "Bíi ril thi le shath wa", eril di be. "Wu sháal!" eril di Shósho. "Radiídin ra; hathalehal sháal hi wa!"

Linguist's Translation
First Line: **Láadan**
Second Line: MORPHEME-BY-MORPHEME
Third Line: Free Translation

Bíide   eril wod i   alehale Shósho   wo.
DECLARATIVE   PAST SIT AND   MUSIC   MAGIC GRANNY   PERCEIVED-HYPOTHETICALLY NARRATIVE.
This is a story I'm telling you, that I made up myself, about once when Magic Granny was sitting and music-ing.

Eril aba   i   owa sháal; eril tháa   déela   betho;
PAST FRAGRANT   AND WARM DAY   PAST THRIVE   GARDEN   HER-OF
The day was fragrant and warm; her garden was thriving.

loláad   Shósho   thena   wo.
PERCEIVE INTERNALLY-   MAGIC GRANNY   JOY-FOR-GOOD- REASONS   PERCEIVED-HYPOTHETICALLY
Magic Granny was very happy, and with good reason.

"Bíi   ril thi le shath   wa,"   eril di be.
DECLARATIVE   PAST HAVE I HARMONY+OBJECT   MY-OWN-PERCEPTIONS PAST SAY SHE.
"To my way of perceiving things, all's right with my world", she said.

---

[1]This lesson originally appeared in a somewhat different form, in *Hot Wire*, March 1986. Used with permission.

"Wu   sháal!" eril di   Shósho.
SUCH-A   DAY!   PAST SAY   MAGIC GRANNY
"Such a day!" said Magic Granny.

"Radiídin ra; hathalehal sháal hi   wa!"
NON-HOLIDAY   NO;   TIME-GOOD-VERY   DAY   THIS   MY-OWN-PERCEPTIONS.
"This is no non-holiday—this is a fandangous day!"

Notes on the Translation:
    English has no verb "to music", but Láadan does. That word "non-holiday" has no English equivalent, but means an alleged holiday when you have to work so hard that it's worse than a working day. "Fandangous" is a better word for "superb".

###

    What I want to do here is change keys. I'm going to give you almost the same story, but with a slightly different vocabulary. You do the translation.

Wohíya Wodedide ShóSho Bethu

    Bíi eril wod I delishe Shósho wo. Eril líithin i modi sháal; eril nótháa déela betho; loláad Shósho shama wo. "Bíi ril thi ra le shath wa", eril di be. "Wu sháal!" eril di Shósho. "Radiídinelh hulehul; harathalehal sháal hi wa!"

Vocabulary:
delishe: TO WEEP
líithin: GRAY
modi: UGLY
nótháa: CEASE TO THRIVE
shama: GRIEF FOR GOOD REASONS, WITH NO ONE TO BLAME, AND NOTHING TO BE DONE ABOUT IT
ra: NEGATIVE, NO
radiídinelh; NON-HOLIDAY + PERJORATIVE
hulehul: FOR-SURE
harathalehal: VERY BAD, SAID OF TIME

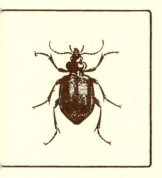

Lesson #2

Aranasha Bethu

Bíi nahóya Aranesha Athileya—nahóyaháalish wa. Memahina abesh; zhe womelíithi woboshum yáanin, i mehel oyimahina reneth óoma netha yil wa. Melirihal babi zhe melirihul mahina. Hotheya woho, láad ne hodoth i lehinath i léelith, woliyeneth wohesheth i woyetheth wohilith. Wu hohama wa! Uhudehóo raden, aril hal ra rawith wa. Thalenhal, owáano—thi Aranesha, Athileya, uhudemid. Wil mehothel uhudemid wa.

Vocabulary:

hoya: BE BEAUTIFUL, (of a place)

liíthi: BE WHITE

uhud: NUISANCE

uhudemid: TICK (NUISANCE-CREATURE)

Athil: APRIL

liri: BE COLORED

that: BE GOOD

hothal: BE BLESSED

Linguist's Translation

First line: Láadan

Second line: MORPHEME-BY-MORPHEME

Third line: Free Translation

Bíi	**nahóya**	**Aranesha Athileya—**	
DECLARATIVE	START-TO-BE BEAUTIFUL	ARKANSAS	APRIL-IN

[2]This less originally appeared in a somewhat different form in *Hot Wire*, July, 1986. Used with permission.

nahoyaháalish   **wa**
START-TO-BE BEAUTIFUL-TO EXTRAORDINARY DEGREE ACCORDING TO MY PERCEPTIONS
incredibly beautiful, to my mind.

Memahina abesh; zhe womelíithi   woboshum   yáanin
PLURAL-BLOOM   ALL-THAT-IS   BE-LIKE REL-PLURAL-BE-WHITE   REL-PL-CLOUD   TREES
Everything is in bloom; the trees are like white clouds,

i   mehel   oyimahina
AND   PLURAL-MAKE   VIOLET
and the violets make a carpet under your feet.

reneth   óoma netha yil   wa.
CARPET-OBJECT   FOOT   YOU-OF   UNDER   MY PERCEPTIONS.
(see above)

Melirihal   babi zhe melirihul   mahina.
PL-BE COLORED-VERY   BIRD   LIKE   PL-BE COLORED-<u>VERY</u> FLOWER
The birds are brightly colored like the flowers.

Hotheya woho, loláad ne hodoth i   lehinath
PLACE-AT   EVERY   PERCEIVE   YOU TULIP-OBJECT AND   LILAC-OBJECT
Everywhere, you see tulips and lilacs

i   léelith, woliyeneth wohesheth i   woyetheth
AND   JONQUIL-OBJ   REL-BE GREEN-OBJ   REL-GRASS-OBJ   AND REL-BE SILVER-OBJ
and jonquils, green grass, and silver water.

wohilith.   Wu   hohama   wa!
REL-WATER-OBJ   WHAT-A   GLORY   MY PERCEPTIONS
What a glory!

Uhudehóo raden, aril   hal ra rawith wa.
NUISANCE-FOCUS   WITHOUT   FUTURE   WORK NOT NOBODY   MY PERCEPTIONS
Without some specific nuisance, nobody would get any work done.

Thalehal,   owáano—thi Aranesha, Athileya, uhudemid
BE GOOD-VERY   THEREFORE   HAVE ARKANSAS   APRIL-IN   TICK
It's a very good thing, therefore, that Arkansas, in April, has ticks.

Wil   **mehothel**   **uhudemid**   **wa...**
LET-THERE-BE   PLURAL-BE BLESSED   TICK   MY PERCEPTIONS
Bless the ticks...

Notes on the Translation:

    1. The title means, literally, "Arkansas It-Of"; "About Arkansas". The word "*Araneshá a*" is a loan word, a "Láadanization" from English.

    2. Láadan has a set of degree markers, including "*-hal*" (neutral "very") and "*-hul*" ("very, to an extreme degree") and "*-há alish*" ("very, to extraordinary degree"); that lets you use the contrast betwéen "*melirihal*" and "*melirihul*" to indicate the both the birds and the flowers are very colorful, but the flowers are more so.

    3. In the sentence about seeing tulips and green grass and silver water, and so on, all the grammatical objects carry the object marker "*-th*" at the end; this is formally correct. However, whether you **must** use the object marker or not depends on your worldview. If you want to say that you speak Láadan (*di le Láadan*, SPEAK I LAADAN), you absolutely don't have to add the marker (*Láadaneth*), because "the language speaks me" is entirely impossible. Similarly, if you were perceiving a book or a chair, you would need no object marker. But can the tulips and lilacs and so on "perceive you" back? If so, the object marker is required to indicate who or what is doing the perceiving. I've put them in to demonstrate; if you don't hold with sentient flowers and grass and water, you can take them back off; thus "you see lilacs" becomes just "*láad ne lehina*" instead of "*láad ne lehinath*".

    4. Some of you may find that "RELATIVE" morpheme mystifying...I suspect it looks like linguist jargon. English derives "the green grass" from "the grass which is green", with "which is green" the relative clause; when a language does that with a morpheme instead of by grammatical processes like moving things around and deleting and inserting stuff, the morpheme is called a "relativizer". So, "*liyen:*" is "be green" and "*hesh*" is "grass"; "*woliyen wohesh*" is "green grass" because of the relativizing prefix.

    5. The focus marker "*-hóo*" was left out of the beginning dictionary (along with many other things, due to space constraints). It is added to a word to mean "this particular specific one" or for emphatic stress—the context will indicate which.

6. You might be interested in knowing a little more about the words for "bridge" and "butterfly". One of the things that women do in their language behavior, in all of the languages I know, is a whole lot of <u>body</u> language work. I wanted that work to be less in Láadan, and the language is therefore constructed to <u>lexicalize</u> body language.

(That is, to give it a pronounced form, instead of leaving it all to be done by tone of voice and gesture and facial expression and so on.) That's why you have the set of words that tell whether the sentence coming up is a statement or question or something else; and that's why you have the endings that tell whether the sentence is meant as a joke or a lesson or a narrative or something else—to reduce the communications labor for the women speaking. The word for bridge, when its tone markers are in the right place, has a sound pattern like this: ___⌐_. The word for butterfly is like this: ⌐_⌐. Since intonation (the melody) that carries the spoken words) is part of body language, this is another way of lexicalizing it. For both of these words, the voice makes the shape of the thing named, in the ear's space and the ear's time. Shapes "in the air", you perceive, but for the ear rather than for the eye.

Lesson 3

Wolaya Wohíya Lub
(The Little Red Hen)

Bíide:

Rilrili wolaya wohíya lub wo. Eril náhalehal be i naya álub bethath i thaáhel be wo. Wemeneya eril di lub, "Bíi aril dala le edeth wa". I mime be, "Báa aril den bebáa leth?" "Bíi ra le hulehul wa!" eril di muda bedim wo. "Bíi ra le hulehul wa!" eril di éesh bedim wo. I "Bíi ra le hulehul wa!" eril di dithemid bedim wo. "Bíi aril hal le sholanenal wi", eril di lub. I eril shub be haleth wo.

Wumaneya eril di be, "Bíi aril róo le edeth i el le baleth wa. Báa aril den bebáa leth?" "Bíi ra le hulehul wa!" eril di muda. "Bíi ra le hulehul wa!" eril di éesh. I "Bíi ra le hulehul wa!" eril di dithemid. "Bíi aril hal le sholanenal wi", eril di lub. I eril shub be haleth wo.

Ihée di be, "Bíi aril nayod le baleth. Báada aril den bebáa leth?" "Bíi aril meden neth lezh hulehul wa!" medi muda i éesh i dithemid. "Bó mewam nezh!" eril di lub. "Bíidi aril meyod le i álub letha baleth—hulehul—wi!" Bíidi eril hinal wo.

Linguist's Translation
First Line: **Láadan**
Second Line: MORPHEME-BY-MORPHEME
Third Line: Free Translation

Bíide: Rilrili (0) wolaya wohíya lub wo.
DEC-NAR   HYP REL-RED REL-LITTLE HEN HYPOTHETICAL
Once upon a time, there was a little red hen.

---

[3]This lesson originally appeared in a somewhat different form in *Hot Wire*, November 1986. Used with permission.

Eril náhalehal   be i naya álub.
PAST   CONTINUE-WORK-VERY   SHE AND LOOK-AFTER CHICK POSS-BY-BIRTH
She worked very hard, and looked after her chick.

i   thaáhel be   wo.
AND   GET-BY   SHE HYPOTHETICAL
and she got by.

Wemenaya eril di lub, "Bíi aril dala le edeth wa".
SPRING-IN   PAST SAY HEN   DEC FUTURE PLANT I GRAIN-OBJ MY PERCEPTIONS.
In the spring, the hen said, "I will plant the grain".

I mime be, "Báa aril   den   bebáa leth?"
AND ASK   SHE Q   FUTURE HELP 3rd PERSON Q   I-OBJ
And she asked, "Who will help me?"

"Bíi ra le hulehul wa!"   eril di muda bedim wo.
DEC NEG I FOR-SURE   MY PERCEPTIONS PAST SAY PIG SHE-TO HYPOTHETICAL
"Not <u>me</u>!" said the pig to her.

[Repeat for "*éesh*" (the sheep) and "*dithemid*" (the cow).]

"Bíi aril hal le sholanenal wi",   eril di lub.
DEC   FUTURE WORK I ALONE-MANNER   SELF-EVIDENT PAST SAY HEN.
"I will do it all by myself", said the hen.

I eril shub be haleth   wo.
AND PAST DO   SHE WORK/ OBJ HYPOTHETICAL.
And she did the work.

Wumaneya eril di be,
SUMMER-IN   PAST SAY SHE
In the summer, she said,

"Bíi aril róo le edeth i el le baleth wa."
DEC   FUTURE HARVEST I GRAIN-OBJ AND MAKE I BREAD-OBJ   HYPOTHETICAL
"I will harvest the grain and make the bread".

[Add "Who will help me?" and as before, they all say "Not me!" and she says she will do it alone, and she does.]

Ihée di be, "Bíi aril nayod le baleth.
LATER   SAY SHE   DEC   FUTURE START-EAT   I   BREAD- OBJ MY-PERCEPTIONS
Later she said, "I'm going to eat the bread.

"Báada aril   den bebáa   leth?"
Q-JOKE   FUTURE   HELP   3rd-PERSON-Q   I-OBJ
"Who will help me?"

"Bíi aril meden neth lezh hulehul wa!"
DEC   FUTURE PLURAL-HELP YOU-OBJ   WE   FOR-SURE   MY PERCEPTIONS
"<u>We</u> will help you!"

medi   muda i   éesha i   dithemid.
PLURAL -SAY PIG   AND   SHEEP   AND COW
said the pig and the sheep and the cow.

"Bó   mewam   nezh!" eril di lub.
COMMAND   PLURAL-BE STILL   YOU   PAST   SAY   HEN
"You just stay where you are!" said the hen.

"Bíidi   aril   meyod, le i   álub letha baleth—hulehul—wi!
DEC-TEACHING   FUTURE PL -EAT   I-OBJ AND CHICK   ME-OBJ BREAD-OBJ   FOR SURE   SELF-EVIDENT
"We will eat the bread, me and my chick!"

Bíide eril hinal wo.
DEC NAR   PAST   THUS   HYPOTHETICAL
And that's the way it was.

Notes on the Translation
1.   The very first line of the Linguist's Translation has a null symbol (∅) in it, as a courtesy to speakers of English. Láadan has no "copula"—that is, no obligatory from of "be" that has to appear; for "she is tired", Láadan, like many other languages, would have just "she tired". The null is where the "be" form would go if Láadan had one.

2.   When the hen asks, "Who will help me?" for the last time, she puts the affix "-*da*" on the question word, "*Báa*". This "-*da*" is the marker that means, "I say this to you only as a joke".

3.   Finally, when she tells the do-nothings she doesn't need their help to eat the bread, the hen adds the <u>teaching</u> affix "-*di*" to the declarative, to let them know that she's hoping they will understand this and learn from it. And the command form "*Bó*" that starts her speech is one used very rarely, and usually for speaking to small children.

Conclusion

We are now at the end of this preliminary grammar. For further materials and information, please feel free to contact me. A tape of this grammar is available for $5.00 postpaid. Also available is a 50-minute videotape, "Suzette Haden Elgin Talks about *Native Tongue* and the Problems of Women's Language", $22.50 postpaid, from the same address.

Suzette Haden Elgin
PO Box 1137
Huntsville, AR 72740

About The Author

Suzette Haden Elgin, Ph. D. is currently Director of the Center for Language Studies, in Huntsville, Arkansas. She was formerly a professor of linguistics at San Diego State University. She received her doctorate in linguistics at the University of California San Diego.

About the Publisher

SF^3 (or, more formally, the Society for the Furtherance and Study of Fantasy and Science Fiction, Inc.) is a not-for-profit Wisconsin corporation with IRS tax-exempt status. SF^3 is the umbrella corporation that sponsors activities like WisCon, an annual feminist-oriented science-fiction convention, and feminist oriented magazines like *Aurora* and *New Moon*.

Notes

Notes